HOISINGTON JUNIOR HIGH SCHOOL

THEY CAME FROM SPACE

BY ELWOOD D. BAUMANN

FRANKLIN WATTS
New York / London / 1977

Photographs courtesy of: Walter R. Aguiar, NYC: pp. 6, 13, 35, 37, 40; United Nations (Rothstein): pp. 18, 19; New York Public Library Picture Collection: pp. 22, 25, 83; Mexican Government Tourist Department: p. 33; Ohio Historical Society: p. 43; British Tourist Authority: pp. 51, 55; Spanish National Tourist Office: p. 57; Centre d'etudes et de Documentation Prehistoriques: p. 59; Arab Information Center: pp. 62, 71; United Nations: 78; French Embassy Press & Information Division: p. 85.

Baumann, Elwood D
   They came from space.

   Bibliography: p.
   Includes index.
   SUMMARY: Presents evidence that suggests many unexplained structures throughout the world are linked to interplanetary visitations.
   1. Interplanetary voyages—Juvenile literature.
2. Civilization, Ancient—Juvenile literature.
3. Man, Prehistoric—Juvenile literature.
[1. Interplanetary voyages. 2. Civilization, Ancient. 3. Man, Prehistoric] I. Title.
CB156.B38   001.9′42   76–44435

Library of Congress Cataloging in Publication Data
ISBN 0–531–00388–4

Copyright © 1977 by Elwood D. Baumann
All rights reserved
Printed in the United States of America
6 5 4 3 2 1

CONTENTS

Mysteries of the Southern Hemisphere	1
Candelabra of the Andes	3
Camels in South America?	3
Spaceman in the Desert?	4
The Giants of El Enladrillado	5
Tiahuanaco—City in the Sky	7
Cuzco—Inca Capital	11
Machu Picchu—Fortress City	17
Easter Island	20
The Short Ears versus the Long Ears— an Easter Island Legend	23
Mysteries of the Northern Hemisphere	33
The Olmecs	36
Cholula	40
The Mayas	41
Mound Builders	44
Giants in Death Valley	46

Dinosaurs in the Grand Canyon — 48
Who Discovered America? — 49

Mysteries of Europe — 53

Stonehenge Mounds — 56
Avebury — 56
Silbury Hill — 57
British Giants — 58
Cro-Magnon Cave Paintings — 59

Mysteries of the East and Africa — 67

The Incredible Maps of Piri Reis — 70
The Visions of Ezekiel — 72
Babylon Rediscovered — 75
The Lost Sumerians — 79
The Queen of Sheba — 81
Zimbabwe—an African Riddle — 83
The Flying Machines of India — 85
The Astronaut of the Sahara Desert — 90

The Gods — 95
Bibliography — 101
Index — 105

THEY CAME FROM SPACE

MYSTERIES OF
THE SOUTHERN HEMISPHERE

While studying ancient civilizations in South America, Dr. Paul Kosok of Long Island University heard about some mysterious lines and figures that had been seen by airplane passengers in Peru's Nazca desert. The descriptions intrigued him, and in 1940 he went off to have a look for himself.

The trip was a disappointment. About all he could see was a confusing jumble of shallow trenches. A top layer of dark pebbles had been removed to reveal the lighter soil underneath. The dark pebbles had then been piled along the edge of the trench, and the contrasting colors formed lines that were quite easy to see.

It wasn't until he flew over the area that Dr. Kosok really got excited. The lines were as straight as an arrow and ran off in all directions. Some were five miles long; others were only a few yards in length. All of them started and ended as abruptly as an airport runway.

But there was far more than straight lines to be seen! Dozens of geometric figures had been laid out with painstaking precision. Scattered among them were drawings of spiders, a nine-fingered monkey, whales, birds, and reptiles. The drawings were so huge that they could only be seen from the air.

Archaeologists who rushed to the Nazca desert were utterly confused. How could the ancients possibly have made these enormous drawings? they wondered. And why would they go to so much trouble to make something that could only be seen from high above? After all, it did seem rather silly to make drawings that they would never be able to see themselves.

Dr. Kosok had his own theory. He believed that the lines were a form of calendar that pointed to positions of the sun and also gave data on the moon, planets, and other heavenly bodies. They marked the passage of the seasons and may have predicted eclipses. The Nazca desert, he wrote, was the largest astronomy book in the world.

Perhaps the most vexing question about the drawings is, How were they done? How could people with no surveying equipment make absolutely straight lines that extended for five miles? How could they make perfect drawings if they weren't even able to see what they were doing? It was suggested by some that the ancient builders must have had outside help of some kind and that the help might have come from somewhere in the sky.

Several students of the Nazca markings became convinced that this was true. Erich von Daniken, a Swiss author and explorer who devotes his life to studying the mysteries of ancient civilizations, bravely declared his belief that this thirty-mile-long level strip of desert had been an ancient airfield. He then went a step further and said that the lines and drawings had been done according to instructions from an aircraft. Alan Landsburg is of the opinion that the lines might have been made to give directions to visitors from outer space. Robert Charroux insists that there were no ancient civilizations in South America that had the scientific or technical knowledge to carry out such a colossal task. It is not on a human scale, he says, so it had to be done by an advanced civilization from beyond our earth. People may have done the actual physical labor, he continues, but the master architect must have directed the work from some kind of aircraft.

Dr. Maria Reiche is the world's foremost authority on the Nazca markings. Since around 1941, she has been living in an adobe hut

Mysteries of the Southern Hemisphere 3

in the desert. Nearly every hour of daylight is spent trying to unravel the mysteries of the lines and drawings. She believes that they are approximately fifteen hundred years old, but admits that she has no idea why they were made. In her book *Secret of the Desert,* she says that the mystery of the Nazca markings is a puzzle that will take scientists many years to solve.

Once the puzzle of the markings has been solved, the scientists can turn their attention to other mysteries near Nazca which are just as intriguing and confusing.

CANDELABRA OF THE ANDES

The Bay of Pisco is about seventy miles northwest of the most northern point of the drawings in the Nazca desert. On one of the sheer cliffs facing the sea, there is a strange carving in the rock. Nobody knows who made it or what purpose it was supposed to serve. It's generally agreed, though, that there's some connection between the giant carving and the Nazca markings.

In some respects, the cliff carving resembles a three-branched candlestick, and it is commonly referred to as the Candelabra of the Andes. This simple description, however, does not allow for the fact that each of the three main branches has smaller branches representing people and animals. The carving is crudely done, but its enormous size alone makes it impressive. The center axis is fifteen feet wide, two feet deep, and over eight hundred feet long.

The gigantic carving can best be seen from two points—from a boat far out in the Pacific, and from the sky. So does this mean that the Candelabra of the Andes served as a sort of marker? Some believe that it did. They think that its purpose was to guide astronauts coming in over the ocean to the landing sites at Nazca. There's no way of knowing whether or not this is true.

CAMELS IN SOUTH AMERICA?

There are other carvings near Nazca that nobody has been able to explain. On the plateau of Marcahuasi there are giant sculptures of human beings, lions, and camels. Certainly, today these animals do not inhabit that region. Did they ever? At least one archaeologist says yes. Peter Kolosimo has found fossilized remains in South America that he says are the bones of camels. The scientific answer to the riddle is that camels became extinct in South America, where they once flourished over a wide expanse of territory. Added weight is given this view by the fact that there are also carvings of camels in Peru.

SPACEMAN IN THE DESERT?

Another puzzle is found nearly five hundred miles south of Nazca at Tarapacá, Chile. A pilot reported seeing a huge figure of a human on the desert floor. Archaeologists went to investigate. All they could see was a line of volcanic stones. It wasn't until they flew over the area that they were able to get a good look. Whoever had drawn the figure must have known that it could be seen properly only from the air.

The outline was enormous. Its overall length was longer than a football field. The human had a rectangular body and a square head. Twelve straight antennae of equal length stuck out from it. Triangular fins resembling the stubby wings on modern supersonic fighter planes were attached to the body.

This was a strange and unworldly figure, it's true, but one thing was perfectly evident. The drawing suggested flight. None of the archaeologists questioned that. Why else had the artist given it a pair of wings?

The question of the twelve prongs sticking out like antennae couldn't be so easily answered. Why were there twelve of them? What purpose did they serve?

A Chilean archaeologist named Salvador Caldera came up with a theory uniquely his own. He suggested that the figure was that of a robot. That brought in another possibility: the robot may have come to earth from an orbiting mother ship or a distant planet. It could have landed in a space vehicle, gathered the needed information and returned to its home base. Modern researchers are gathering data from other worlds, so it's possible that an advanced civilization used robots to do the same thing on earth in ages past.

Archaeologists trying to solve the mysteries of unknown civilizations in South America were faced with some rather tough problems. Travel was difficult in the sky-scraping Andes, and the early stages of the work were usually carried out from the air. If something of interest was sighted, they would have to go in on foot or on horseback for a closer look. The trouble, though, was that some objects that showed up clearly on photographs could barely be seen by observers on the ground. In one case, giant sculptures of human beings, animals, and birds were sighted high on a Peruvian plateau. Archaeologists who rushed to the spot were completely dumbfounded. There was nothing at all to be seen! They were beginning to believe that they had come to the wrong place when one of them made an amazing discovery. The carvings were there all right, but they were only prominent when the sun shined on them from a particular angle.

THE GIANTS OF EL ENLADRILLADO

In 1968, another chapter was added to the list of still unsolved mysteries of South America. Reports of some unusual formations on the plateau of El Enladrillado in northern Chile reached the outside world, and an expedition led by Humberto Bounaud went up to have a look.

Everything the expedition encountered defied logical explanation. Parallel lines of volcanic rocks stretched across a perfectly level part of the plateau. The lines were approximately one thousand yards long and about sixty-five yards apart. Not far from this, there were 233 volcanic blocks weighing as much as twenty thousand pounds each, and all of them had been cut into rectangular shapes. It was impossible to tell whether the ancient builders had completed or were still building a broad avenue, a landing strip for aircraft, or something entirely different.

There were other mysteries. Carvings on the nearby cliffs portrayed animals that looked like nothing ever seen in South America.

A giant carved head from the Copan ruins in Honduras

A large statue of a man with distinctly European features was found lying on its face in the brush. There were also two twelve-foot-high altars and a number of enormous stone seats. Indian legends told about a race of giant gods that had once lived on the El Enladrillado plateau, and at least one member of the expedition suggested that the legend might be true.

Humberto Bounaud refused to go along with the giant theory. He believed that an ancient unknown culture had been at work on the plateau. That culture, he said, may have come from the skies or perhaps was expecting visitors from outer space. The unknown beings who lived on the plateau, he declared, must have known that the place would make an ideal landing ground for all kinds of flying bodies.

So the mystery of the plateau of El Enladrillado remains unsolved. One archaeologist suggests that it's the work of a race of giant gods. Another believes that an unknown civilization from another world may have been at work there. And still others scratch their heads and say that they simply don't know who could have performed such a monumental task.

Neither do they know how, or when, or why.

TIAHUANACO—CITY IN THE SKY

The mightiest ruins in all South America are near Lake Titicaca, high in the Bolivian Andes Mountains. Nobody knows who built the city and no one knows how old it is.

It's difficult to believe that Tiahuanaco could have been built by human beings alone. "Even gods and giants would have a tough time building a place like this," a Canadian engineer said when we were photographing the ruins one bitterly cold day.

I asked him if modern engineers could construct anything similar and he shook his head. "No. No, we couldn't," he said slowly and thoughtfully. "The people who built Tiahuanaco knew something that we don't know. Our technology would break down before we even got started on a project like this."

I wasn't surprised. Tiahuanaco is a staggering sight. It lies on an inhospitable plateau about thirteen thousand feet above sea level.

The soil is infertile and there isn't a tree anywhere in sight. Icy winds sweep down from the towering, snow-capped Andes. Clouds and mist shroud the area for days at a time. It is a desolate wasteland, yet an unknown civilization built a majestic city on this unfriendly, sky-high plateau.

Tiahuanaco teems with unsolved mysteries. All of the stonework has been finished to perfection. Blocks weighing one hundred tons are topped with sixty-ton blocks. The surfaces are smooth and the great blocks have been fitted together with such precision that the blade of a knife can't be forced between them. Many blocks have ten or more corners, yet the fit is always perfect.

A jumble of stone heads in a courtyard represents several different races of people. Some of the faces have thick lips and others have thin ones. There are faces with straight noses and faces with hooked noses. Some faces are angular and some have soft, round features. Heads with curly hair can be seen as well as heads with straight hair. Nearly every race on earth seems to be represented, but how would people living on a remote South American plateau have known that these distant races even existed?

The Gate of the Sun at Tiahuanaco is one of the world's greatest archaeological mysteries. It was cut from a solid slab of greenish-gray andesite, an extremely hard volcanic rock found only in the Andes Mountains. It is ten feet high and twelve feet wide and weighs about as much as five bull elephants. Over eleven hundred figures or symbols have been carved on the front of the gate.

What strange secret is locked in this incredible stone frieze? What story is told by this amazing array of sculptures? There are carvings of winged figures, human heads, birds, and animals that have been extinct for millions of years. Forty-eight figures in three rows surround a flying god. Some of the figures are wearing a curious headgear not unlike the space helmets worn by today's astronauts.

Archaeologists from all over the world have tried to decipher the inscriptions on the Gate of the Sun. One scholar, Dr. Arturo Posnanski, spent thirty years studying the symbols, then declared them to represent a calendar showing the four seasons, the solstices, and the equinoxes. According to Posnanski, the calendar has the years divided into ten months of 24 days, and two months of 25 days. Each day has 30.2 hours and there are 290 days to a year. This meant that each year was 8,758 hours long. Our year today has 8,760 hours, or only 2 more hours per year than the Tiahuanaco calendar. The scientist published his findings in a 433-page book and solemnly declared that the mystery of the Gate of the Sun had been solved.

Not everyone agreed. Alexander Kazantsev, a Russian scientist, insisted that the inscriptions were actually a calendar of the planet Venus. He managed to prove to his own satisfaction that the calendar showed that one day on Venus was equal to nine days and seven hours on earth.

Some scientists believe the Gate of the Sun tells the history of Tiahuanaco. Still others believe that it is a message from one unknown people to another. There is one point, though, on which most of them agree: The concept of flight appeared to be known to this ancient civilization. Robert Charroux even states that Tiahuanaco may have been one of the world's first space bases.

Anyone who has visited Tiahuanaco finds it quite easy to believe that the builders were very interested in several aspects of flight. There are figures of flying gods, and one statue weighing more than twenty tons appears to be wearing a space suit. A strange device on the statue's chest may be some sort of a control box. Scientists from America, Russia, and France agree that several of the figures on the Gate of the Sun closely resemble spaceships.

Those who favor the theory that Tiahuanaco was built by aliens from another world have a number of arguments to support their theory. They believe that the space travelers made the South American plateau their home base. The space people expected to be joined by others, and the Candelabra of the Andes and the markings on the Nazca desert and on the plateau of Marcahuasi were carved to help guide them in from the sky. Like the Apollo crew on the moon, they pinpointed landmarks as navigation aids and studied the possibility of establishing a permanent base sometime in the future.

Tiahuanaco could not have been built by an ancient Andean civilization, say those who believe the space visitor theory, because the barren and inhospitable plateau on which it is located could never have supported a large population. There simply wouldn't have been enough food for everyone. An estimated one hundred thousand men would have needed several generations to build a city like Tiahuanaco. In addition to the men, there would probably have been at least two hundred thousand women and children. This meant a total population of nearly a third of a million people. Vast fields of grain and large herds of livestock would have been needed to feed the populace, but the barrenness of the plateau would have made this impossible. Even finding enough wood for a fire would have been a serious problem.

The other problems the builders would have faced were just as difficult to solve. The best engineers, in fact, still can't solve them today. Many of the stones came from a quarry ninety miles away —but how could blocks of stone weighing fifty tons or more have been moved such a distance across rugged country? And how could these gigantic blocks have been shaped and grooved to an accuracy of within a fraction of an inch? No tools or other implements have ever been found at Tiahuanaco, so there are no clues.

Archaeologists can only guess at the age of Tiahuanaco, and their guesses vary dramatically. Hans Bellamy, author of *Built before the Flood,* says that Tiahuanaco must be at least 250,000 years old. In *The Calendar of Tiahuanaco,* author Percy Allen says that the city was built many tens of thousands of years ago. Dr. Arturo Posnanski estimates the city's age to be between 16,000 and 18,000 years. There are also scientists who boldly declare that the city was built as recently as 1,000 years before the birth of Christ.

Not only are scientists unable to agree on the age of Tiahuanaco, but they have different opinions as to what happened there. Although their theories cannot be proved, they make interesting reading.

Hans Horbiger, an Austrian scholar, studied the inscriptions on the Gate of the Sun and, like Posnanski, declared that the figures represented a calendar. But Horbiger claimed the gate showed there were only 290 days in a year. The years were shorter, we are told, because the moon was at that time farther from the earth. This was about fifteen thousand years ago and the moon was not the same one that we see now. The world was very much different then and Tiahuanaco was a thriving seaport.

As the years passed—according to Horbiger's theory—the moon's orbit around the earth kept getting smaller. The closer the moon came to the earth, the more rapidly the earth rotated on its axis.

And then one day it happened! Something went wrong in the universe and the moon smashed into the earth. The force must have been equal to that of millions of nuclear bombs. There were volcanic eruptions, earthquakes, gigantic storms, and cosmic bombardments. Entire civilizations were wiped out in a second. The oceans of the world were freed from the moon's forces and the water dropped thousands of feet. Instead of being a seaport, Tiahuanaco found itself stranded in midair two hundred miles from the sea.

Another school of thought also believes that Tiahuanaco was once a busy seaport, but it rejects the theory that the moon collided with the earth. This school states that a violent cataclysmic upheaval lifted the city some 2½ miles up into the air. The same force that created the Andes in South America also created the Rocky and Cascade mountains in North America, the Alps in Europe, and the Himalayas in Asia.

Dr. Arturo Posnanski, Alexander Kazantsev, and other experts agree that Tiahuanaco was once a seaport. They claim that they are able to point out the remains of wharves and anchorages. They also claim to have traced the old shoreline and found seashells and other evidence of marine life. The water in Lake Titicaca is salty, and there are numerous salt deserts in the region. They say this proves that the lofty Bolivian plateau was once the bottom of the ocean and maybe they're right.

This is an interesting bit of information, it's true, but it leaves the most important questions unanswered: Who were the mysterious people who built Tiahuanaco? How did they do it, and when? Where did they come from, and what happened to them?

So far, we don't have even the slightest clue.

CUZCO—INCA CAPITAL

Francisco Pizarro, the conqueror of Peru, entered the Inca Empire in 1532 with 178 armed men. To the surprise of the Spaniards, they were warmly welcomed by the natives. An ancient legend said that bearded men from the east had once lived among the Incas. They had gone back to their home beyond the sea, but they had promised to return at some time in the future. That promise, the welcoming Incas believed, had at last been fulfilled.

This tragic misunderstanding is easily explained. The natives of South America had no facial hair. Until the arrival of Pizarro and his band of conquistadores, none of them had ever seen a man with a beard. Their legend, however, told that the bearded men from the east were good men, so the Andean Indians were naturally glad to see them back.

It wasn't long before the unfortunate Indians realized that there was nothing good or godlike about their visitors. They were cruel and treacherous men and they soon proved it. Atahualpa, the Inca emperor, was at the town of Cajamarca with his army when the Spaniards arrived. Pizarro presented his respects to the emperor and invited him to dinner. There was no reason to refuse the invitation. The Inca army was camped in the area and the Spaniard had only a handful of men. There was nothing to worry about. The escort that accompanied the emperor to Pizarro's dinner was unarmed.

The two men seem to have had only one thing in common: Neither of them could read or write. Francisco Pizarro was illiterate because he had been sent out to herd swine while still a small boy and had never been to school. Emperor Atahualpa was unable to read or write because the highly civilized Incas had no written language.

The dinner at Cajamarca was the beginning of the end of the mighty Inca Empire. Atahualpa had accepted the invitation in good faith. He had no reason to suspect his bearded host, but his innocent trust proved to be his ruin. During the course of the meal, Pizarro suddenly leaped to his feet and ordered his men to attack.

Atahualpa was made a prisoner of the Spaniards, and his men were massacred. Muskets and cannons roared. Volley followed volley and a hail of lead smashed into the Inca army. The ground ran red with blood. The unsuspecting soldiers of the emperor never had a chance. Several thousand Indians were slaughtered before the guns finally fell silent. Those who had survived the massacre returned to their homes.

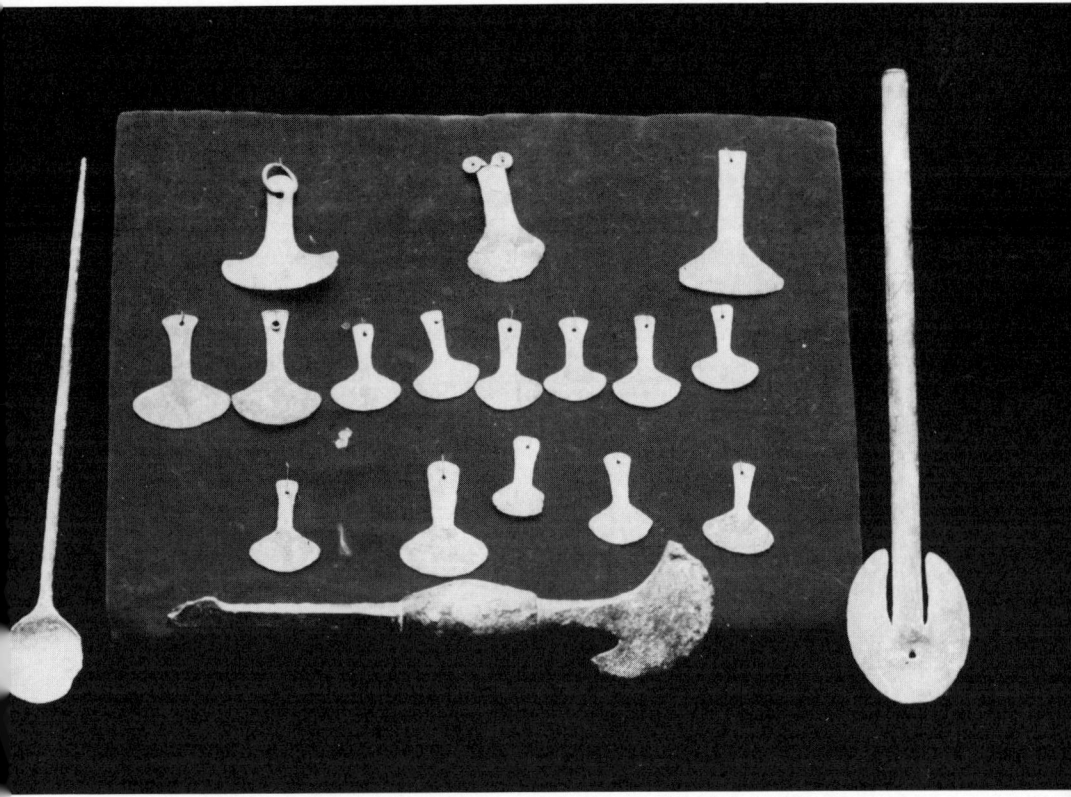

Inca surgical tools

It's very fortunate that not all of the Spanish conquistadores were as ruthless and unenlightened as Francisco Pizarro. A number of them realized that the Incas were a truly remarkable people. Not even in their wildest dreams had the Spaniards expected to find anything as awe-inspiring as the Inca Empire. They marveled at their achievements and sent detailed reports back to Spain.

The illiterate Andean Indians had developed an incredibly advanced level of civilization. Inca doctors successfully performed operations that are still considered difficult today. Dentists made and fitted false teeth. Farmers built terraces, dug irrigation ditches, and used fertilizer to enrich their crops. Engineers designed and built fortresses and cities that must be seen to be believed.

Even the most unimaginative of the conquistadores must have

been deeply impressed by Cuzco, the capital of the Inca Empire. Nobody could possibly have expected to see such a fabulous sight in the wilds of the Peruvian Andes. There was no other city on earth like it. The population of the capital was estimated to be approximately two hundred thousand, larger than any city in sixteenth-century Europe.

A high wall of immense stones enclosed Cuzco. The approach was guarded by the mighty fortress of Sacsahuaman. Every building had running water, and water flowed through dozens of beautiful gardens. The working class lived in its own section of Cuzco, but there were no slums. The palaces of the nobles were in the city center and the temples were everywhere. There were approximately four hundred of them and they were all magnificently constructed. It was the fabulous Temple of the Sun, however, that really delighted the greedy Spaniards.

Perhaps the best description of this lovely building is given in W. H. Prescott's *History of the Conquest of Peru*.

> The interior of the temple was the most worthy of admiration. It was literally a mine of gold. On the western wall was emblazoned a representation of the Sun God, consisting of a human face looking forth from amidst innumerable rays of light which emanated from it in every direction in the same manner as the sun is often pictured for us. The figure was engraved on a massive plate of gold of enormous dimensions and thickly powdered with emeralds and other precious stones.

The Spaniards had no respect at all for the religion of the Incas. They cared only for gold and jewels and they ruthlessly plundered every bit of it that they saw. The Temple of the Sun was stripped of everything of value and so were all the other temples in Cuzco.

Next to the Temple of the Sun, the most impressive place in Cuzco was the fortress of Sacsahuaman. Although no gold was found there, the Spanish invaders were awed by its enormous size. The same thing is true of people who visit the fortress today. How, they invariably ask, could anyone have built such a gigantic structure? That's a very good question and the archaeologists would very much like to know the answer.

Even the cannons of the Spaniards could not have inflicted any damage on Sacsahuaman. The wall around it is sixty feet high and fifty-four feet wide. Many of the stones in the wall weigh well over one hundred tons and all of them are of flint-hard andesite. They are fitted together with an incredibly high degree of precision. The only entrance to the fortress was through doors on the top of a mountain that had been artificially leveled.

The Incas' system of communications may not have been as spectacular as their capital and fortress, but it was certainly impressive. Their vast empire stretched from what is now Colombia in northern South America all the way down to central Chile. The total area was approximately 350,000 square miles. The population was somewhere around two million people. A good system of communications was needed to hold such a great empire together and the Incas had the best in the world.

The Romans boasted in their days of empire that all roads led to Rome. All the roads in the Inca Empire led to Cuzco and they were much better than the Roman roads. There was one surprising difference, however. Chariots zipped along at top speed on their way to the capital of the Roman Empire, but there were no chariots on the roads to Cuzco. The Incas didn't have chariots, either because they had no animals or people to pull them or because they didn't know about the wheel. Llamas refuse to pull carts, but men can move heavy loads on wheeled vehicles. It's quite possible, then, that the Incas didn't make use of the wheel because they didn't know about it.

Building a road in the Andes is still considered to be a tough job, but it must have been much tougher for the Incas. They had no surveying equipment, no earth-moving machinery, and no explosives. In spite of the handicaps, they built magnificent roads. The main highway through the empire stretched a distance roughly the same as that between New York and San Francisco and was between twenty-four and twenty-five feet wide. Branch roads ran down to the Pacific coast, to the steaming jungles east of the Andes and to any settlement of importance. There were rest houses or inns at twenty-mile intervals.

The greatest part of the main highway ran through almost impossibly difficult terrain. Passes higher than the highest peaks in our Rocky Mountains had to be crossed. Roaring rivers and dizzying gorges had to be bridged. Cliffs of solid rock had to be tunneled through and the surface of the road always had to be kept as smooth as possible. This presented endless problems, because the rocks had to be properly shaped before being fitted into the road surface. It's certain that nobody has ever counted the number of rocks it took to build the main highway, but it must be many, many millions.

The communications system perfected by the Incas was surprisingly swift. Messages carried by young men running in relays could cover a distance of 1,250 miles in five days. Deliveries from the Pacific coast to Cuzco were faster four centuries ago than they are today. Relays of Inca runners brought fresh fish and fruit from the coast to the capital daily and the trip was made in just over twenty-four hours. Cuzco is two miles above sea level, so it was uphill almost all the way.

Until the sad days of the Spanish invasion, everything in the Inca Empire had to be transported either on llamas or the backs of men. Horses and mules were brought in from Spain, but they weren't brought in to make life easier for the unlucky Indians. They were brought in to carry the plundered gold and silver from the Andes down to the Pacific Ocean. Historians estimate that over a billion dollars worth of treasure was looted from the Incas, carried to the coast and shipped to Spain.

Although the Incas achieved a very high level of civilization, they never developed a written language. The ruling class partially overcame this handicap very nicely, however, by employing professional "rememberers." These rememberers used a device called a quipu to help them keep a record of events. Knots of various sizes were tied into strings of different colors. Each knot represented a certain happening, and a series of strings would be a sort of history

Other authorities suggest the quipu was a mathematical device, with knots representing numbers. The colorful string was used to record numbers in a decimal system. A translator, says this theory, had to accompany each quipu to decipher it.

The quipu was a brilliant invention. Territorial governors used the rememberers to record all events of importance. The strings were sent to the capital each year and this enabled the emperor to know how things were in the provinces. Mathematical problems could also be worked out on the quipu and the Spaniards were amazed at the speed and accuracy with which the problems were solved.

Whoever invented the quipu must have been a person of genius. Everything the emperor wanted to know was recorded on a series of knotted multicolored strings.

Unfortunately, the quipu had one great disadvantage: It could only be read by a rememberer, and the last of the professional rememberers died over four centuries ago. Bundles of gaily colored strings can still be seen in museums, but nobody knows how to decipher them.

MACHU PICCHU—FORTRESS CITY

The most famous fortress city in South America is Machu Picchu. It was discovered in 1912 by the American explorer, Hiram Bingham. The Spaniards never saw it and they wouldn't have been interested. Machu Picchu is a splendid sight, but no gold was found there.

Machu Picchu is perched on a small plateau high in the Andes. The Urubamba River foams and froths three thousand feet below. Parts of the steep cliff were terraced for agriculture, and the Indian farmers faced a most peculiar danger. If they got careless, they could fall out of their cornfield and be killed.

Bingham's discovery excited the scientific world. A lost city had been found and perhaps some of the questions about the Incas could now be answered. But no such luck! The discovery of Machu Picchu only deepened the mystery. Nobody could imagine why they had built their fortress city in such a remote and inaccessible spot. Were they protecting themselves from some enemy, or were they hoping to make contact with the gods? Machu Picchu can easily be seen from the air, but persons on foot must be almost inside the city before they can see it.

Building Machu Picchu must have been a staggering task. The giant blocks of stone came from quarries several miles away. What if they had to be hauled across the swiftly flowing Urubamba, then brought up a steep cliff three thousand feet high?

How could this be done? The river roars through a narrow

Machu Picchu ruins in Peru

gorge and would be too much for even the strongest swimmer. No bridge built by the Incas would have been sturdy enough to support the weights of the massive stones. The fact remains, though, that they *did* get these blocks of stone across the river, and all the way up the cliff to the site of the city.

There are some scholars who think they know how this was done. Their theory might sound terribly fantastic, but it's really no more fantastic than Machu Picchu itself. The Incas, they believe, knew how to defy the laws of gravity. In some manner or other, they managed to make the stone weightless. Perhaps they even made them float in the air so that they could easily be pushed across rushing rivers and up steep cliffs.

A segment of the huge Inca fortress of Sacsahuaman in Peru. The fortress once guarded the approaches to Cuzco, the Inca capital.

We don't dare to scoff too loudly at this theory, because it just might be true. Antigravitational research is being carried out at a number of universities, and evidence points to the fact that sound waves may be used to overcome gravity. If gravity is completely overcome, then an object supposedly becomes completely weightless.

Scientists have still not been able to prove any connection between sound and weightlessness, but some ancient writings spur them on. For example, inscribed tablets found in Babylon declared that sound could lift stones. Priests were able to raise heavy rocks high into the air by the use of their voices alone. The Bible tells us that the sound of Joshua's trumpet brought the walls of Jericho tumbling down. Coptic writings found in Egypt said that blocks for the pyramids were lifted into place by the sound of chanting. If the Babylonians and Egyptians were able to defy gravity, then isn't it possible that the Incas were able to do the same thing?

That, of course, brings up the next question: How were the Incas with their crude tools able to cut these huge rocks out of the cliffs and fit them together with such precision? Some archaeologists think that they may have the answer to that one, too. They are of the opinion that these ancient builders had developed some method of making stones as soft as putty. Once the stones had been placed into position, they could be molded into the shape desired and left to harden.

Colonel P. H. Fawcett, the great South American explorer, related an interesting incident he had heard from some American mining engineers in Peru. They had found a sealed container in a burial mound and placed it on a large rock. The container was broken accidentally and a liquid spilled out. To the amazement of the engineers, the surface of the rock soon became so soft that they were able to knead it with their bare hands. Although Fawcett concluded that the rock-softening liquid came from certain jungle plants, he was never able to identify them.

And that's where the matter rests today. The Incas may have been able to move the huge blocks of stone effortlessly because they knew how to overcome gravity. They may have been able to shape and position the blocks so accurately because they had a liquid that would soften them. Unfortunately, we don't know exactly how these Andean Indians built their enormous structures, because their genius died with their empire.

EASTER ISLAND

Easter Island is a small and lonely speck of land in the Pacific Ocean. It is an area about sixty-five square miles. A few hundred people live there. One of the strange things about the island is that it has almost as many statues as people.

The statues are enormous. Many weigh thirty to fifty tons and stand higher than a house. One giant is just a fraction over seventy

Mysteries of the Southern Hemisphere

feet tall. All of them were originally placed on stone platforms with their backs to the sea.

Jacob Roggeveen, a Dutch admiral, discovered the island on Easter Sunday, 1722, and named it Easter Island. The admiral, it appears, was not a very imaginative man. He admitted that the enormous statues intrigued him, but he refused to believe that they were actually carved from rock. The natives had no metals, no heavy rope, and no wood for rollers, so they could not possibly have carved the statues, transported them across the island, and set them up on their platforms. The statues, he declared, had to be made from clay.

Not until the last half of the twentieth century did a fully equipped archaeological expedition attempt to solve the mystery of Easter Island. The leader of the expedition was Thor Heyerdahl, the Norwegian adventurer who had sailed a boat named the *Kon-Tiki* from Peru to Polynesia. Olav V, king of Norway, was the expedition's patron.

"Señor Kon-Tiki," as the natives called Thor Heyerdahl, soon learned that he had a big job in front of him. There were over six hundred giant statues on the island. Most of those which had been completed had been pushed off their stone platforms and were lying on their faces. Others were nearly finished, partially completed, or just barely begun. Crude stone tools lay about the ground. It seems that work on the statues had stopped suddenly.

The problems faced by the expedition were enormous. How, they asked one another, had Stone Age people with flimsy stone tools carved these enormous statues out of solid rock? How had they moved them from the quarry at one end of the island to the stone platforms at the other end? And how had they stood them up on the platforms?

The Easter Island people had answers of their own. They simply stated that either their ancestors or someone else had carved the statues. And when a statue had been completed, it left the volcanic crater and walked downhill to the platform that had been built for it. There it stayed until it fell over onto its face.

Heyerdahl was convinced that the ancestors of the present-day islanders had carved the statues with primitive stone hammers and chisels. The statues had then been rolled to their platforms on

Easter Island heads

wooden rollers. To get the giants into position, they had used long poles, lengths of heavy rope, and every able-bodied man on the island.

Some scientists insist that people with crude stone tools could not have carved the hard volcanic rock into a twenty-ton figure. Their tools, say the doubters, would not have been equal to the task. The population of Easter Island, they add, had never been large enough to provide the number of workers needed to carve so many statues. Estimates as to the time it took to carve a single statue varied widely, but it was generally agreed that even several generations of islanders working full-time could not have carved six hundred of them.

Some scientists also take exception to Heyerdahl's theory of how the statues had been transported and erected. There had never been any decent-sized trees on Easter Island, the scientists say, so there wouldn't have been any wood for the rollers or the poles. (There were trees on Pitcairn Island, but that meant a voyage of twelve hundred miles, which was out of the question. Driftwood, in fact, was a very precious commodity on Easter Island and not a scrap went to waste.) The same thing was true of ropes. The natives could not have used ropes for pulling the statues into an erect position because there was nothing on the island from which thick and heavy ropes could be made. Neither could the wood and ropes have come from neighboring islands.

The Short Ears versus the Long Ears—
an Easter Island Legend

When the early explorers visited Easter Island, they found wooden tablets hanging from the necks of some of the statues. The tablets were covered with a type of writing that was totally unfamiliar to them. The visitors asked the islanders what the writing meant, but not a single person was able to read it.

The first European to settle on Easter Island was Brother Eugène Eyraud, a Catholic missionary. He had come to bring Christianity to the natives, but he went about it in rather a strange way. For reasons known only to himself, he decided that the wooden tablets were sinful and evil things. They had to be destroyed, he said, and most of the islanders did as they were told. Fortunately, however, a number of the tablets had already been carried away to the outside world. A few more were hidden in caves on the island.

The experts who studied the wooden tablets were completely baffled. The writing was unlike anything they had ever seen before. It was beautifully inscribed in straight lines. The words of one line were written from left to right and those on the line below were written from right to left.

Every effort to decipher the writing ended in failure. No one was able to make heads or tails of it. The wooden tablets very possibly held the secret of Easter Island, but they stubbornly refused to reveal any clues. Tribal warfare and slave raids had wiped out the ruling class and there was nobody left on the island who could read the strangely beautiful writing.

But who were these people who had developed a system of writing? Had they also carved these giant statues? Where had they come from? Thor Heyerdahl asked these questions of the islanders and became convinced that he had found the answers.

A legend said that the first people to reach Easter Island had come from the west. They had spent sixty days sailing in the direction of the setting sun. This meant that they must have come from the South American mainland, nearly twenty-five hundred miles away.

Heyerdahl believed that there was a certain amount of evidence to support this legend. Huge stone statues had been carved by several different civilizations in South America. Roads similar to those on Easter Island could be seen in the Andes Mountains. Both the Easter Islanders and the Peruvian Indians called the sweet potato *kumara*. The Inca ruling class pierced their earlobes and forced wooden plugs into the slits to make the lobes longer. Most of the statues on the island had unnaturally long earlobes, and the legend said that the first settlers also had long ears.

That, however, was only the beginning of the legend. A century or so later, it went on, another group came to settle on Easter Island. They came from islands far to the east. They were smaller and darker than the first settlers and they all had short ears. The people with long ears soon forced the people with short ears into

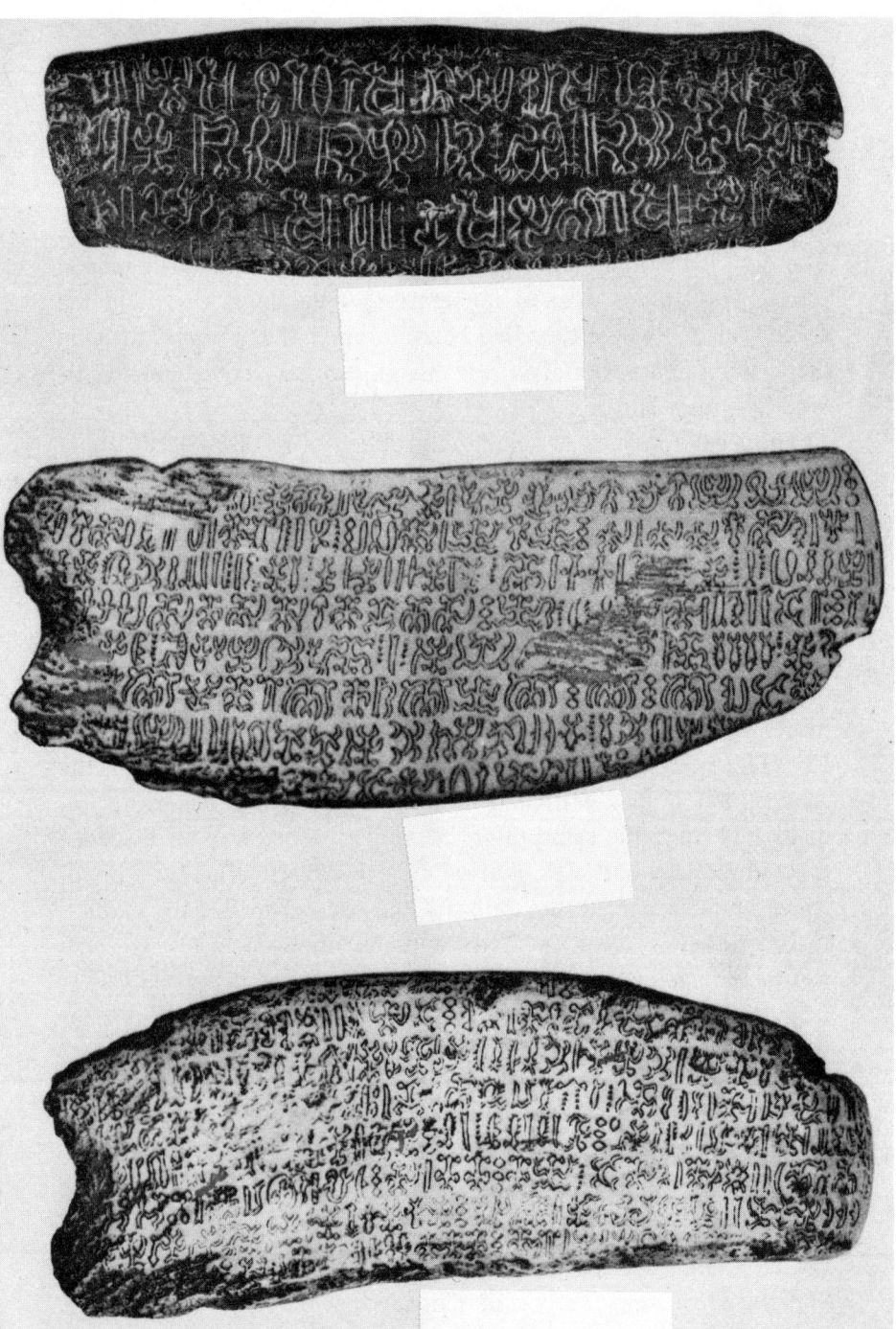

Easter Island writing stone

slavery. The short ears were set to work carving statues and the long ears supervised the work.

Then came the day of reckoning! The short ears suddenly rebelled and the battle was on. They drove their enemies to the tip of the Poike peninsula and slaughtered every last one of them. The day of the long ears was over and Easter Island was again at peace. The statues were of no interest to the short ears, and the stone tools lay where they had been dropped. They were still lying there when Señor Kon-Tiki and his expedition arrived on the island a century later.

The legend seemed to solve the problem of the islanders' origin. It also explained why the work on the statues had stopped so suddenly. Again, some anthropologists and archaeologists accepted Heyerdahl's theory and others refused to accept it. The skeptics did not believe that the first settlers had come from the South American mainland. They pointed out that the Peruvian Indians were not seafarers. Their tremendous surf made sailing extremely hazardous; there were very few islands close to the mainland, and few places suitable for a harbor. It was true, of course, that Señor Kon-Tiki had sailed a balsa raft from Peru to the South Pacific islands, but it was extremely doubtful that South American Indians had done the same thing. Moreover, there was no evidence that the Indians had ever used sails on their rafts. The early Spanish explorers reported that the rafts had been propelled by paddles.

The disbelievers did not attach much importance to the same words, such as *kumara,* being used in South America and on Easter Island. There had been contact between these two civilizations for well over a century before Heyerdahl's arrival.

What about the long earlobes? The skeptics had an answer for that, too. While it's true that some South American Indians stretched their earlobes, it's also true that many South Sea islanders also stretched theirs and still do so today.

It was virtually impossible to convince any of the scientists that Easter Island had been settled by South American Indians. L. Sprague De Camp, author of *Citadels of Mystery,* for example, insists that the natives of Easter Island definitely arrived there from other islands in the Pacific. There is no chance at all, he declares positively, that the short, copper-skinned, straight-haired

Peruvian Indians evolved in a few centuries into the tall, brown-skinned, wavy-haired Polynesians. The Polynesians, he continues, were some of the greatest seafarers in history. On the other hand, there is no evidence that the South American Indians ever ventured very far out to sea.

All of the scientists agree that Thor Heyerdahl is a courageous and imaginative adventurer. Very few of them, however, believe that he has solved the mystery of Easter Island.

When something on our earth cannot be explained, there are always people who will come forward with a theory. Some of the theories make a certain degree of sense; others are inclined to be pretty farfetched. De Camp's theory on the history of Easter Island seems to be one of the more sensible ones.

The author of *Citadels of Mystery* believes that boredom was the islanders' worst enemy. They lived on one of the loneliest places in the world. No ships ever anchored in their little harbor. They saw the same faces day after day, year in and year out. Nothing ever changed. The diet of seafood and sweet potatoes seldom varied. Life was easy, but terribly boring. There was practically nothing to do and each day was almost the same as the day before.

Boredom led to quarrels and the quarrels led to feuds and open warfare. One side would emerge victorious and the victors would go back to their same old way of life. A few people tried to keep themselves occupied by making signs and figures on rocks or pieces of driftwood. The figures and signs gradually took on meaning, and a written language eventually evolved.

Those who had no interest in a written language turned their attention to other things. Perhaps it was sheer boredom that prompted the natives to build roads on their island. It may very well have been a bored islander who strolled over to the Rano Raraku crater one day and began chiseling away with his stone tools. The idea of carving a statue may have occurred to him after a while, and he kept at it month after month until it was completed. There was nothing else to do anyway and carving a statue helped to pass the time.

The other islanders wandered over to see the statue and they decided that they wanted one, too. Theirs, of course, would be bigger and better and they began to chip away with all their might.

The days now passed quickly. There was work to do and the sound of hammering was heard in the crater at all hours. Life became an exciting challenge. No longer were the men satisfied with only one statue apiece. They wanted two or three, or ten or fifteen each. The men later formed themselves into groups so that they could carve even bigger and better statues.

It was the arrival of white men that brought work on the statues to a sudden stop. In 1862, several Peruvian ships dropped anchor off the island. Soldiers rushed ashore and attacked without warning. Some people were killed and about a thousand were carried off as slaves. The bishop of Tahiti heard about the outrage and persuaded the Peruvian government to return the captives to Easter Island. Only fifteen of the captives lived to see their homes again and all of these had been exposed to smallpox. The disease spread rapidly and the population of the island dwindled to 111 inhabitants. Work on the statues was never resumed and the system of writing was lost forever.

Erich von Daniken has an entirely different theory. He will not accept the general belief that the statues were carved by natives using crude stone tools. Carving, transporting, and erecting the statues, he says, would have been an impossible task for the native Easter Islanders.

If the natives of Easter Island could not have carved the enormous statues with their crude stone tools, then they must have been carved by someone else. That someone else either possessed ultramodern tools or a technique of working stone that is still not understood today. They must also have known something that we don't know about moving great weights. Had the carvers of the statues been able to defy the laws of gravity?

Von Daniken attempts to answer such questions. He accepts a wildly fantastic Easter Island legend as fact. The legend says that men from the sky once visited Easter Island. Von Daniken suggests the space travelers developed spaceship trouble and were forced to land in the Pacific Ocean.

There may be several reasons, von Daniken continues, why the visitors decided to carve the statues. They may have thought that the islanders would like them, or perhaps they wanted to leave a lasting memory of their stay. It's also possible that the statues were a sign to the people who would come looking for them. The wooden tablets that had hung from the statues' necks may have told about their stay on the island, or they may have described the world in space from which they had come. The writing on the tablet, you'll remember, was unlike any writing ever seen anywhere else on earth.

The day of rescue came at last. The ailing spaceship was repaired and the space travelers blasted off into the blue. It was a sad time for the islanders. They had enjoyed helping the men from the sky work on the statues. They had chipped cheerfully away with their stone hammers and chisels while their visitors performed miracles with ultramodern equipment.

Now their friends were gone. There was no sense in trying to carve any more figures with their puny stone tools, so they tossed them aside and went home. After all, they had over six hundred giant statues on their little island and that ought to be enough for anyone.

Erich von Daniken admits this theory sounds fantastic, but Easter Island is an utterly fantastic place.

MYSTERIES OF
THE NORTHERN HEMISPHERE

Thirteen years before Pizarro landed in Peru, Hernando Cortes and his band of conquistadores landed in Mexico. Montezuma, the Aztec ruler, sent gifts to the Spaniards and hoped for the best. His astrologers had told him that Quetzalcoatl would return to reestablish his rule, and this information worried Montezuma greatly.

Quetzalcoatl was one of the most important gods in Mexico. Legend said that he had brought peace, prosperity, and happiness to the people. He taught them law, healing, writing, and many other things that would make life easier for them. Then he sailed away in the direction of the rising sun. Before leaving, however, he told his people that he would return again in the same day of his birth to rule over them once more. His birth had been on the Aztec day of One Reed which would recur in the Christian calendar year of 1519. It was in 1519 that bearded men from the east landed on the shores of Mexico.

The identity of Quetzalcoatl is shrouded in mystery. Nobody knows who he was or where he came from. Neither does anyone know whether he was actually a god or simply an especially brilliant leader of his people. "We can assume that this mysterious figure, part myth and part man, once lived," stated Victor von Hagen in *Aztec: Man and Tribe.*

Other writers have not been so cautious. W. Raymond Drake says that Quetzalcoatl came from outer space and insists that there is much evidence to support his theory. Harold T. Wilkins and Marcel Homet believe that he came to Mexico about 11,000 B.C. from the sunken continent of Atlantis. Hyatt and Ruth Verrill believe that he arrived from Babylon before 2000 B.C. Constance Irwin, author of *Fair Gods and Stone Faces,* suggests that Quetzalcoatl was a Phoenician god who reached Mexico about twenty-five hundred years ago.

Montezuma's advisers begged him to declare war on Cortes and his men, but the ruler was hesitant. If the strangers turned out to be gods, then all would be lost.

It wasn't long before the Aztec people were thoroughly tired of their uninvited guests. They realized that there was no trace of resemblance between Cortes and Quetzalcoatl. The Spaniards were interested only in gold, jade, emeralds, and the pretty Indian women. The Aztec people wanted to have the Spaniards destroyed. Montezuma, however, was still undecided. He tried to reason with the people, but they had had enough. The Aztecs suddenly rose up against the strangers. Cortes and his men were driven from the city after bitter fighting. Montezuma was murdered by his own people.

The sounds of battle were soon heard again on the high Mexican plateau where Tenochtitlán, the Aztec capital, was located. Tribes unfriendly to the Aztecs joined forces with Cortes, and Indians and Spaniards marching side by side attacked the capital. Cannons roared, gunfire rattled, and a thousand fires swept through the streets. The city that Cortes had described as one of the most beautiful sights in the world was utterly destroyed in the attack. Only the charred ruins of temples and pyramids remained. The death of Montezuma and the destruction of Tenochtitlán in 1521 marked the beginning of the end of the brilliant Aztec civilization.

Quetzalcoatl, the mysterious god they had worshiped with such fervor, had deserted them.

Several of the men who accompanied Hernando Cortes on his

The Aztec Calendar Stone

triumphant march through Mexico wrote detailed reports on what they had seen. They described the splendors of the capital and the grandeur of Montezuma's court. The order and cleanliness of the cities impressed them. The enormous temples and pyramids came as a complete surprise. None of the conquistadores, it seems, had expected to find such a highly advanced civilization in the New World.

More than four and a half centuries have passed since Cortes began his conquest of the Aztec nation, but scientists are still studying the history of these remarkable people. Many decades of archaeological search have turned up a wealth of information, and more is being learned each year. And more and more mysteries which still haven't been solved keep popping up all the time.

Twenty-five hundred years before the Aztecs attained any degree of power, an unknown number of other cultures had already been established on Mexican soil. Several of them had reached a high level of civilization, but tribal warfare had weakened some and wiped out others. When the Aztecs became the rulers of Mexico, they also acquired much of the knowledge that had been accumulated over the centuries by the nations they conquered. This knowledge was of immense value to them and they made the most of it.

THE OLMECS

The Olmecs were one of the earliest, most talented, and most mysterious civilizations in the New World. Their influence was felt throughout much of Mexico. Dr. Matthew W. Stirling of the National Geographic Society says that they gave ancient Mexico its first great cultural impetus. The effects of this impetus, he states, lasted until the conquistadores of Cortes brought it to a sudden end over two thousand years later.

Dr. Stirling spent eight years doing archaeological research on the Olmecs in southern Mexico. He calls them America's first great artists, and he has good reason to. One of the works of art he discovered was a massive stone head. It was nine feet long and weighed thirty tons. The huge block of stone from which it had been carved had come from a quarry more than sixty miles away across rugged mountainous country. "The enterprise, patience and skill required to perform this feat could be the product only of an unusual civilization," wrote Dr. Stirling in the *National Geographic Magazine* of February 1947.

Just how unusual were the Olmecs? And what kind of people were they? A total of eleven huge heads was discovered by Dr. Stirling and all of them had the same features: broad foreheads, flaring nostrils, thick lips, and narrow slits for eyes. They bear no resemblance at all to any race of people that has ever lived in the Americas. "These enormous heads, in appearance more African

An Olmec head

than Indian," wrote Charles Berlitz, "are one of the New World's greatest and oldest mysteries."

Indian legends told about a race of giants who had once lived in Mexico. They had built pyramids and temple-cities and carved statues and other figures. Could these giants, then, have been the Olmecs? Were the giant stone heads found by Dr. Stirling actually the heads of giants? Nobody knows, but altars more than six feet high were uncovered in Olmec country and it would take a very tall man to worship at an altar of that height.

The fact that all the Olmec heads were wearing helmets confuses the issue even more. The helmets fit the head closely and come down almost to the level of the eyes. What purpose they were supposed to serve is unknown. Dr. Stirling says jokingly that he may have unearthed eleven helmeted members of an Olmec football team. W. Raymond Drake, on the other hand, suggests seriously that the Olmecs may have been visited by men wearing space helmets. We don't know who is closer to the truth, but we have to admit that a thirty-ton stone head wearing a helmet is something very difficult to explain.

Excavations at Monte Albán in the state of Oaxaca in Mexico revealed another statue that confounded the archaeologists. This one wasn't nearly as impressive as the giant stone heads, but it was just as much of a mystery. The statue is of a bearded man in a squatting position. He is wearing a turban and nothing else. There is a look of complete peace on the man's face and he is definitely not an Indian. He appears to be a nice gentle old fellow of about sixty, but there is nothing at all godlike about him.

It's not even possible to make an intelligent guess as to the man's identity. We don't know where he came from or how he got to Monte Albán. The turban suggests that he might have come from Egypt or Babylonia, but how could he have gotten to Mexico many centuries before the New World had been discovered?

The "Dancers' Gallery" at Monte Albán is totally unlike either the stone heads or the turbaned statue. These stone carvings show strange-looking men who seem to be doing a clumsy version of a ballet. They appear to be wearing space helmets and space suits. There are fastenings that look somewhat like zippers on the arms and thighs, and the curious shoes they are wearing turn up at the toes.

All of Monte Albán, in fact, is a most mysterious place. The ancient builders not only built a city, but they also redesigned the

A figure from the so-called Dancer's Gallery

surrounding countryside. Forests were uprooted, the top of a mountain was hacked away, and terraces covering thousands of acres were made. Massive blocks of stone were brought from distant quarries to construct the temples, pyramids, tombs, and other buildings in the city.

Dr. Alfonso Caso, a Mexican archaeologist who has spent most of his life studying Monte Albán, believes that the city was founded by the Olmecs about 1000 B.C. At that time, they had already developed a form of writing and had a surprisingly accurate calendar. Other cultures occupied the city at later dates. They made many changes, but the Olmec influence is still there. Nearly everyone agrees that the Dancers' Gallery, the statue of the bearded man wearing a turban, and the carved inscriptions on the stone pillars are unmistakably Olmec. Unfortunately, the inscriptions cannot be deciphered, or the whole mystery of this strange city might be solved.

CHOLULA

Cortes and his conquistadores fought a great battle at Cholula on their way to the Aztec capital. At that time, it was a beautiful city of about 150,000 inhabitants. The city was founded by the Olmecs, but it was ruled by Montezuma when Cortes arrived in 1519.

Cholula must have been a great religious center. There were temples to all the gods, and Cortes reported in a letter to King Charles V of Spain that he had counted over four hundred pyramids. By far the largest one was dedicated to Quetzalcoatl.

If the historians are correct, it was the most colossal edifice on the North American continent. It covered forty-two acres and was 210 feet high. Millions of bricks had been used in the construction, and its mass was greater than that of the Egyptian pyramid of Cheops. A magnificent temple on the top of the pyramid housed a giant image of Quetzalcoatl, and pilgrims came great distances to worship him.

Von Hagen says that Quetzalcoatl himself ordered the great pyramid to be built, and it's quite possible that the god actually was in Cholula at one time. W. H. Prescott, the noted authority on the conquest of Mexico, states that the image of Quetzalcoatl in the temple on top of the pyramid shows him "with a black skin unlike the fair complexion which he bore upon earth." There is no explanation for this, but it should be remembered that the giant stone heads discovered by Dr. Stirling were more African than Indian in appearance.

THE MAYAS

The great Maya civilization lay far to the south of Teotihuacán and Cholula. The name of their chief god was Kukulcán, which like Quetzalcoatl means "feathered serpent." Legends said that he came from the east and established his capital at Chichén Itzá in Yucatán.

As in the case of Quetzalcoatl, it is difficult to know whether Kukulcán was actually a man or merely a myth who developed into an important god. Certain scholars believe that Quetzalcoatl led his people south from Cholula to Yucatán where he was given the Mayan name of Kukulcán, but his exact identity is as much of a mystery as Quetzalcoatl's. They might have been the same man—or myth—or they might never have existed at all.

The conquistadores were not impressed with the highly advanced Maya civilization. They were interested only in treasure and they massacred and destroyed in their relentless search for it. Priests and the ruling class were put to the sword. Cities were razed to the ground. Entire libraries were destroyed and only three books in the Maya language are in existence today.

Although the Mayas were never completely conquered by the Spaniards, their spirit and civilization were broken. Their magnificent cities were swallowed up by the jungle. Nearly three hundred years went by and history almost forgot the fact that an advanced culture had once thrived in southern Mexico and Central America. Then this lost civilization was rediscovered by two adventurous young men.

"Modern Maya archaeology," states Dr. Michael D. Coe in *The Maya,* "stems from the epic journeys undertaken between 1839 and 1842 by the American diplomat and lawyer, John Lloyd Stephens, and his companion, the English topographical artist Frederick Catherwood, which revealed the full splendor of a vanished tropical civilization to the world."

Stephens's book, illustrated beautifully with Catherwood's drawings, was an immediate success. Everyone wanted to know more about this brilliant and mysterious race of people who had built such fantastic cities.

There were many, of course, who refused to believe that these

Stone warriors carved by the Toltec people. By 1200 A.D. their civilization had waned. It was legend by the time the Spanish arrived in Mexico.

cities had been built by Indians. Theories as to who had built places like Tikal, Palenque, Copán, Chichén Itzá, and Bonampak were a dime a dozen. There were pyramids in the cities, said some, and this proved that they had been built by Egyptians who had somehow found their way to the New World many centuries ago. Not so, said others. These pyramids were not at all like those in Egypt. They resembled those found in southeast Asia, so the builders must have come from Cambodia or Siam. There were those, too, who were convinced that the Mayas were Vikings. Or Carthaginians. Or Phoenicians. A few identified them as the Lost Children of Israel, one of the tribes that had disappeared without trace centuries before the birth of Christ. There were some, too, who insisted that the Mayas were survivors from the continent of Atlantis which had sunk beneath the waters of the Atlantic. These people could not accept the fact that the Mayas were simply an unusually advanced Indian nation.

In recent years, a new and rather surprising theory has been put forward. Men like Erich von Daniken, Alan Landsburg, Peter Kolosimo, W. Raymond Drake, Charles Berlitz, Andrew Tomas, and a host of other writers boldly proclaim that many of the ancient civilizations were so advanced only because they had received help from people or gods from outer space. We don't know whether this is the case or not, but this theory is certainly an interesting one.

These writers present their accumulation of "proof" in a convincing manner. The giant helmeted stone heads and the space-suited figures in the Dancers' Gallery at Monte Albán mean there must have been some sort of knowledge of spacemen, they maintain. The statue of a bearded man wearing a turban also proves to them that the ancient Indians were in contact with people from another world. Many of the carvings suggest flight and one found in the Maya city of Palenque is actually quite startling. It is remarkably similar to photographs of American astronauts about to be launched into space. Erich von Daniken believes that the astronaut is Kukulcán and calls him the Rocket-Driving God of the Mayas.

The most detailed description of the carving is given in Drake's *Gods and Spacemen in the Ancient West*.

> The person whom we see on the sculpture and whom we call The Pilot wears a helmet and looks toward the prow of the ship; his hands are occupied and seem to maneuver levers; his head leans on a support, an inhalator penetrates his nose. On the prow we find three receivers which accumulate energy and other "capturers" forming three series; three on the right, three in the front and three on the left. The motor is subdivided into four parts, the ship's propulsion system is housed behind the pilot. The thrust is clearly visible and is shown in the form of a flame at the rear end of the rocket.

The Palenque carving has aroused a storm of controversy. Are the champions of the visitors-from-outer-space theory letting their imaginations run wild, or was it the imagination of the ancient Indian artist that ran riot?

Or were ancient civilizations actually visited by people from outer space?

At the present time, these are questions which still cannot be answered.

MOUND BUILDERS

In the United States, settlers and explorers who marched east toward the Mississippi River came upon thousands of mounds made by people. Some were flat-topped; others were in the forms of humans or animals.

One person who tried to learn the meaning of the mounds was Thomas Jefferson, the third president of the United States. There was a large mound near Charlottesville, Virginia, that aroused his curiosity. Jefferson was a scientist as well as a statesman and he approached his task systematically. "I proceeded to make a perpendicular cut through the body of the mound," he wrote, "so that I might examine its internal structure."

Unfortunately, Jefferson's mound contained nothing of interest. It was simply a large earthen pile. There were no bones, tools, pottery, or anything else inside.

The great majority of present-day archaeologists agree that the mounds were built by Native Americans. The earliest ones date back to around 6000 B.C. Other mounds were constructed as recently as one thousand years ago. Some were built as burial places and some as raised sites for temples. Several seem to have served as astronomical observatories, and others as elevated platforms for the homes of chiefs. Those shaped like humans or animals are called effigy mounds. At one time, there were approximately twelve thousand of them in Wisconsin alone.

Like many of the works of advanced ancient civilizations, the effigy mounds can be seen more clearly from high above. The early Americans didn't have airplanes, but they may have seen aircraft of some kind. Bird Mound in Wisconsin resembles a plane as much as a bird and the same thing is true of the Eagle Mound in Georgia. A copper plate of a winged man was plowed up in a Missouri field and a carving found in Oklahoma showed a man dressed like an eagle. Some mounds were built in strange geometric designs.

The most mysterious mounds of all are found along the coasts of South Carolina, Georgia, and Florida. They are circular and made

Great Serpent Mound, Adams County, Ohio. The mound was built by Native Americans of the Adena culture.

entirely of saltwater shells. A shell ring on Sapelo Island, Georgia, is more than three hundred feet across and seven feet high. Archaeologists freely admit that they don't have the faintest idea why these shell rings were built or what possible meaning they could have.

A special type of pottery was often found inside the shell circles. It was made of clay and strengthened with vegetable fiber. Many of the pieces were decorated with peculiar patterns of triangles, rectangles, circles, and other geometric forms. Exactly the same kind of pottery was found inside rings of seashells on the Colombian coast of South America.

Was this a coincidence, or were Indians from North America in contact with Indians from South America? Did Indians from what is now South Carolina paddle their canoes down to Colombia, or did the Colombian Indians paddle up to South Carolina? All of this happened about four thousand years ago and nobody knows who visited whom. It seems safe to assume, however, that the two cultures knew of each other's existence. What isn't known is why anyone would want to build circular mounds of seashells.

Archaeologists have proved that prehistoric Indians were great travelers. Obsidian knives from Wyoming were found in mounds in the Ohio Valley, more than a thousand miles away. Shells from the Gulf Coast and copper nuggets from the northern Great Lakes area were also found in the same mounds. Implements chipped from Ohio flint have been dug up in Florida and Georgia. Trade routes extended from the Rocky Mountains to the Atlantic Ocean and from the Great Lakes to the Gulf of Mexico.

One of the most important trading centers was located near East Saint Louis, Illinois. Historians call the center Cahokia, and it was the largest city north of the Rio Grande. It had hundreds of mounds and an estimated population of thirty thousand. Monk's Mound, the largest one left, is one hundred feet high and covers sixteen acres. Cahokia even boasted a pyramid, but it was built of earth and was already crumbling away when the first explorers saw it. Unfortunately, the historians have been unable to find out who built the pyramid, because it is not mentioned in any known Indian legend.

GIANTS IN DEATH VALLEY

There are certain mysterious things in the southwestern United States that simply cannot be explained. One of them is found in California's Mojave Desert and is known as the Mojave Maze. This is a confusing tangle of neatly cut trenches and rows and ridges of small stones. It covers many acres and in certain respects is similar to the markings in the Nazca desert in Peru.

Why anyone would dig a complex pattern of trenches and make

long ridges of stones on the floor of the desert is something that defies explanation. It wouldn't have been done without a reason, but what could that reason possibly be? Archaeologists don't know and neither do the Mojave Indians. The Mojaves insist that the maze was not constructed by their ancestors. It was there when the tribe came to the desert, they say.

The mystery of the Mojave Maze deepened when planes began crossing the area. Enormous figures of human beings were then seen for the first time. They had always been there, of course, but they couldn't be seen from the ground.

This presented a pretty problem for the scientists. Being cautious by nature, they didn't want to say that the maze and the figures had been constructed by the same people. They couldn't prove it, so they couldn't say it. They agreed, however, that it would have been difficult to construct the huge figures without some sort of supervision from above.

And there's another point upon which they agree: The figures can't be seen from the ground. The builders didn't know that planes would be flying over the area sometime in the future, and that leads us to believe that they must have had something else in mind. It would be very interesting to know what that something else was.

The giant human figures and the mystery of the Mojave Maze aren't the only things in California that baffle the scientists. Rock carvings found in Death Valley, Inyo County, and Santa Barbara add greatly to the confusion. The carvings are of gods, stars, sheep, lizards, and birds. Others are of triangles, diamonds, spheres, wavy lines, and straight lines. Still others are a meaningless tangle of odds and ends that make no sense to anyone.

Authorities argue about the age of these carvings, but they have come to no conclusions. They can't even be certain that all of them were done by the same civilization. The fact that they were all found relatively close together is their only similarity. There are no legends to help guide the archaeologists and no tools have been found that might serve as a clue to the time when these mysterious carvings were made. When asked how old he thought the carvings were, one scientist simply said, "Oh, they're very old. They're very, very old indeed."

Erich von Daniken, Alan Landsburg, and other writers suggest that the mysteries in California are somehow connected with space travel. The maze and the figures may be a type of landmark for incoming aircraft. The unexplained carvings may be the artist's impression of the interior of a spaceship or of things taken from it. Von Daniken also makes another interesting observation. He believes that the carvings which the archaeologists say are gods are not really gods at all but beings from outer space.

DINOSAURS IN THE GRAND CANYON

The most remarkable rock carvings on earth were reportedly found in Arizona's Grand Canyon. In *Gods and Spacemen in the Ancient West,* W. Raymond Drake states that the Doheny Expedition of 1923 discovered a carving of a dinosaur on a canyon wall. The enormous creature was standing erect, its huge jaws open wide. Not far away was a rock carving of a giant human being fighting a mammoth.

Dinosaurs, giants, and mammoths! Now what can we possibly think of something like that? Dinosaurs have been extinct for millions of years. Mammoths lived during the Ice Age. And giants? Although we don't really know very much about them, stories of races of giants appear in many legends of ancient civilizations. In his book *Stranger Than Science,* Frank Edwards declares that skeletons of giants twelve feet tall have been dug up in California and Arizona. Unfortunately, he doesn't tell us whether or not the skeletons are on exhibit anywhere.

All of us have seen pictures of dinosaurs and mammoths. Scientists have unearthed their skeletons and reconstructed them. Is it possible, then, that prehistoric men and women might have done the same thing?

Or perhaps they found skeletons that were still intact. These told them what the creatures looked like. The huge beasts were intriguing, and so they carved images of them on the canyon wall in order for their friends to see them. The giants were no problem. They were merely abnormally large people and carving one wouldn't have been terribly difficult.

WHO DISCOVERED AMERICA?

Many people now believe that America was discovered two thousand years or more before Columbus was ever born. These early travelers probably came from a Mediterranean or Atlantic culture and may have ventured as far west as the Mississippi. Charles Berlitz in *Mysteries from Forgotten Worlds* gives some interesting evidence to support this theory.

Twenty-two stone structures lay in ruins on top of Mystery Hill, in Salem, New Hampshire. There were tunnels, underground chambers, and buildings of enormous size all laid out in rather a haphazard style. Jonathan Pattee was the first American to settle on the hill and he used the underground chambers and tunnels as storage rooms. The buildings were of no interest to him and a number were torn down and the stones carted off to build the sewers of Lawrence, Massachusetts.

People finally realized that Mystery Hill was a genuine mystery, and what remained of the ruins was taken over by the New England Antiquities Research Association. Robert Stone, director of the operation, declared that the buildings had been constructed in approximately 1000 B.C. In certain respects, they resembled prehistoric structures found on the Iberian Peninsula and on several Mediterranean islands.

The letters or symbols carved on the ruins seemed to be Phoenician in origin. The Phoenicians were great traders and courageous seafarers. They established colonies in a number of Mediterranean lands and it is known that they sailed as far west as the Azores. If others sailed even farther west, they would have landed on the shores of America.

Other letters that closely resembled the Phoenician or a similar alphabet were discovered in Mechanicsburg, Pennsylvania, in 1948. About one thousand grooved stones were uncovered and each one had a single letter carved on it. Scholars who studied the stones suggested that they had been cut to fit together according to alphabetical coding.

In 1885, an inscribed stone was found near Morgantown, Tennessee. It was believed at first that the inscription was in Cherokee. An alphabet for this language had been created by a Native American named Sequoya. Dr. Cyrus Gordon of Brandeis University, however, was given the stone for studying in 1970 and he believed otherwise. He is an authority on ancient civilizations and languages and it was his opinion that the inscription was in Canaanite, the language of a land that bordered on Phoenicia and had a similar alphabet. Another inscribed stone found in Georgia was identified as Minoan by Dr. Gordon. The Minoan civilization flourished on the Greek island of Crete many centuries before the time of Christ, and like the Phoenicians, they were courageous seafarers.

A discovery in Assawompset Pond, Massachusetts, proved to be as big a puzzle as Mystery Hill and the inscribed stones. The level of the lake dropped dramatically during a severe drought and revealed a carving of a ship on an enormous boulder. Historians who studied the vessel believed that it was either Phoenician or Minoan. Geologists said that the lake had been much smaller thousands of years ago, so the stone had been on dry land when the ancient artist carved the inscription.

Great civilizations like the Incas, Mayas, Aztecs, and Olmecs never flourished in our country, but unknown men left us the Mojave Maze, curious rock carvings, giant human figures, and a host of other mysteries which have still not been solved.

And perhaps they never will be. . . .

MYSTERIES OF EUROPE

Stonehenge, the best-known prehistoric monument in Great Britain, stands in bleak isolation on the Salisbury Plain. Its main feature is a cluster of giant stones. Some are standing alone and some are capped by lintels forming great archways. A few of the giant stones are leaning, some have fallen, and many are missing altogether.

It is believed that Stonehenge was built between the years 1900 B.C. and 1600 B.C. Dr. Gerald S. Hawkins, a professor of astronomy at Boston University and author of *Stonehenge Decoded,* is of the opinion that work on the site was begun by a Late Stone Age people and was completed by people who were in contact with the advanced civilizations of Greece, Egypt, Minoan Crete, and Phoenicia. It has even been suggested that master builders may have come to Britain from one of the Mediterranean cultures to supervise the construction of Stonehenge.

Professor Hawkins is convinced that Stonehenge was an astronomical observatory. Inside the circle of standing stones were five archways. A ring of fifty-six holes in the ground, called the Aubrey Holes, surrounded the circle of upright stones. The professor made his observations from the center of Stonehenge and came to the conclusion that the purpose of the site was to align the archways, stones and holes with the sun and the moon.

After making accurate charts of Stonehenge, Hawkins returned to the United States and fed his information into a computer. The answer he got was the one he had expected. The computer told him that Stonehenge was also a computer. It was so advanced that it gave Professor Hawkins some information neither he nor other astronomers had known. The ancient Stonehenge computer told Hawkins that eclipses of the moon take place in cycles of fifty-six years. Somehow or other, the prehistoric builders had acquired an incredible amount of astronomical knowledge.

The construction of Stonehenge was an enormous task. It was built over a period of three centuries by hundreds—or perhaps thousands—of workers. The best and brightest brains in the land did the planning and engineering. Brute force did the rest. Hawkins estimates that the actual construction required the staggering total of 1.5 million days of physical labor.

Eighty-two bluestones form the inner circle of Stonehenge, and these can be found only in the Mynydd Prescelly, mountains in Wales. The average weight of the bluestones is four tons and all of them had to be moved over three hundred miles across land and water. It is generally believed that rafts were used for the water part of the journey and log rollers or sleds for the part across the land. Regardless of how it was done, though, it must have been a tough job to move a four-ton stone so great a distance.

Handling the original thirty huge sarsen stones which formed the outer circle was a much tougher job. Their average weight is twenty-eight tons and some of them weigh fifty tons. Fortunately, these did not have to be brought over from Wales. The sarsens came from the Marlborough Downs, about twenty miles to the north. Nevertheless, Hawkins says that "the task of moving the sarsens to Stonehenge would have kept a thousand haulers busy for seven full years."

After the huge sarsens had been stood upright in the holes dug for them, the workers were ready for the toughest task of all. That task was to place the large flat stones that form the lintels on the

Stonehenge

top. The lintels are about fourteen feet above the ground and weigh about six tons each. Getting them into place must have been a very tricky business and nobody knows for certain how it was done.

There were originally thirty-five lintels in the outer circle, but only a few of them are still in place. The others fell when the upright stones toppled over in ages past.

There is a great deal about Stonehenge that is still unexplained. It isn't known why certain holes and ditches were dug and then filled in. And the positions of certain stones make no sense to the archaeologists.

Professor Hawkins suggests that Stonehenge may also have been a memorial or a place of worship or a meeting place or a combination of all of these things plus many more. He describes Stonehenge as "puzzle heavy" and says that the answers to many of the questions about its origin and purpose may never be found.

STONEHENGE MOUNDS

Much of the mystery of Stonehenge actually lies outside the great circles of standing stones. There are smaller stone circles, mounds, ditches, and avenues. One avenue is nearly two miles long and stops at the Avon River.

The mounds were burial places and are either circular or cigar-shaped. There are nearly 350 burial mounds within twenty miles of Stonehenge and one of them is the largest prehistoric tomb in England. It is 350 feet long and tapers in width from about 100 feet on one end to about 50 feet on the other. When this mound was excavated recently, thirty skeletons were found huddled together at one end with a few pottery vessels. The rest of the tomb had been crammed with rubble.

In *Mysterious Britain,* Janet and Colin Bord suggest that these cigar-shaped mounds may be a form of message to people in the sky. They also note the similarity between the shape of the mounds and cigar-shaped spaceships that have been reportedly sighted.

AVEBURY

The best known of Stonehenge's neighbors is a huge complex of stones at Avebury, just seventeen miles north. A great bank of earth and a ditch surround the entire area. From the bottom of the ditch to the top of the bank is fifty-five feet. A circle of sarsen stones weighing up to forty tons is inside the bank of earth. Today, part of the village of Avebury is also built across the old circle complex.

Archaeologists have had a tough time of it at Avebury because many of the stones were broken up and used to build the village houses and garden walls. Some were pushed over for no reason at all, and one unimaginative farmer had several dozen of the stones dragged into the great ditch because he thought his cows didn't like them. Avebury is older than Stonehenge, and Professor Hawkins thinks that some of the stones may have been taken south and used there. About the only stones remaining are those too big and heavy to be moved. The site is now protected by the Department of the Environment, but the damage has already been done and Avebury will remain an unsolved problem.

Although very little is known of Avebury itself, archaeologists are convinced that it was once a meeting place of the utmost importance. Traders and adventurers from other lands visited there, and it may also have been a religious center. Avebury was at the southern end of a prehistoric road called the Icknield Ridgeway, so it must have been an important spot.

SILBURY HILL

Another great mystery lies within sight of the prehistoric road and just over a mile from Avebury and sixteen miles from Stonehenge. It's called Silbury Hill and it's the largest artificial mound in Europe. The base of the mound covers 5½ acres, and archaeologists estimate that about three million days of work were required to create it. In other words, one hundred persons working every day of the year would have needed more than eighty years to build Silbury Hill.

The popular belief is that Silbury Hill is a burial mound. Legend says that King Sil is buried there on horseback, but nobody seems to know whether or not there ever was such a person. Other versions of the legend tell of a life-size figure of solid gold, of a man in golden armor on horseback, and of a king buried in a golden coffin. Some think that the designer of Stonehenge or Avebury may be buried there, but Silbury Hill is older than either one of these sites.

In 1777, scholars attempted to find out what the mound contained. A shaft was dug from the top straight through to the level of the ground. A lot of hard work was involved, but nothing was found. Another attempt was made in 1849. This time a tunnel was dug from the bottom of the mound to connect with the shaft that had been dug seventy-two years earlier. Once again, the workers came away empty-handed. The purpose of this monstrous earthwork remains a complete mystery.

BRITISH GIANTS

Perhaps the most intriguing figures of all are those carved on the British hillsides. One of them, the Long Man of Wilmington, on Windover Hill in Sussex, is the second largest representation of a human figure in the world. He is 231 feet high. His arms are outstretched and appear to be holding two long staffs. There is no evidence at all of his identity, but some think that the figure is connected with sun worship, and that guess is probably as good as any.

The Cerne Abbas Giant is on Giant Hill in Dorset. Although this giant isn't as tall as the Long Man of Wilmington, he's a mighty big fellow and looks dangerous. He is holding a club in his right hand, and a cloak is draped over his outstretched left arm. There are countless legends of giants in Britain and many people believe that the carving may be of a giant king or a giant warrior. It is also believed that giants are buried in some of the cigar-shaped burial mounds.

The Gog Magog Giants are in the Gog Magog Hills near Cambridge. Mr. T. C. Lethbridge, an archaeologist, had heard that there was a giant figure on one of the hills and he went to investigate. At first, he could see nothing. The entire area was covered with brush. After clearing a part of the hillside, however, he finally found what he was looking for. In fact, he found a bit more than that. Instead of one giant figure, he found three of them. They were Gog, Magog, characters from ancient British mythology, and an unidentified figure of a man wielding a weapon.

Lethbridge's task was a tough one, because he couldn't study the scene properly from the ground. He had to fly over it and take aerial photographs. It was only then that he was able to make an educated guess as to what he had found.

His interpretation of the scene was that the demon of darkness had been stopped by Gog, the sun god, while trying to stop the progress of the moon. Magog, the goddess, was 120 feet high. She

The Westbury White Horse. Carved into the face of a chalk hill, the horse is one of England's mysteries.

appears to be wearing goggles and a type of helmet and is driving a chariot drawn by a horse with a nose like the beak of a bird. The scene is a very confusing one and even Lethbridge readily admits that his interpretation may be far from the correct one.

CRO-MAGNON CAVE PAINTINGS

One summer afternoon in 1879, Don Marcelino de Sautuola and his five-year-old daughter were strolling around on his estate near Altamira in northern Spain. Part of a hillside had recently been blasted away by construction workers, and the mouth of a cave could now be seen. The entrance had been hidden by fallen rocks many centuries before.

While her father was poking around in the rubble, the little girl strolled into the cave. Suddenly she called, "Bulls, Daddy! There are some bulls in here! Come quickly!"

Don Marcelino scrambled through the opening and looked to where his daughter was pointing. In the dim light of the cave, he could see large figures painted on the walls and ceilings. They weren't bulls, however. They were prehistoric bison.

The Spaniard was wild with excitement. He hurried home for a lantern, then rushed back to the cave. His discovery was even more startling than he had at first believed. There were seventeen paintings of bison and they were unbelievably lifelike. Some were standing still. Others were pawing the ground, rolling in the dust or curled up in sleep. All of them had been beautifully painted in shades of black, brown, yellow, and red.

As Don Marcelino explored deeper in the cave, he found dozens of other animals painted on the walls and ceilings: a delicate female deer, giant cattle, stags with enormous antlers, and charging wild boars. Don Marcelino's excitement increased with each discovery. He knew that the paintings had to be very, very old indeed. A number of them were of animals that had been extinct for thousands of years.

A year after his discovery, Don Marcelino published a comprehensive report on the cave paintings. If he had expected the scientific world to share his excitement, however, he must have been bitterly disappointed. Archaeologists read his report and chuckled knowingly. Those who came to Altamira to examine the paintings pronounced them a hoax. It was absolutely ridiculous to think that such superb art could have been created by a bunch of savages, said these learned scientists.

There must have been times when the unfortunate Don Marcelino wished that he had never followed his daughter into the cave. Neither the Spanish government nor any scientific organization was interested in the paintings. They insisted that cave dwellers, people thought to be crude and primitive, couldn't have painted so well, and that was it. Don Marcelino himself was accused of hiring an artist to forge the paintings at Altamira. He was called a fraud and a phony. The Congress of Prehistorians unanimously condemned him.

Perhaps we shouldn't judge scientists too harshly. After all, the

An Altamira cave painting

paintings did come as a severe shock. It had simply never occurred to anyone that cave dwellers might have been talented artists. And it *is* hard to picture a cave dweller painting animals on the ceilings and walls. Where would they have gotten paints and brushes? The cave was dark, so they must have had some form of illumination. They must also have used scaffolding, because the ceiling was so high that they couldn't have reached it from the ground.

No, the idea of a talented cave artist was just too idiotic to be taken seriously. Everyone refused to believe that the paintings were genuine and Don Marcelino died an object of ridicule in 1888.

The cave discovered by Don Marcelino is today one of Spain's most important tourist attractions. A road has been built to the mouth of the cave and floodlights have been installed inside. Tens of thousands of people come to Altamira every year to see the paintings, most of which are still in perfect condition.

Archaeologists now agree that the pictures were painted during the Ice Age by Cro-Magnon people over thirteen thousand years ago. They lived in caves, because it was only there that they could find protection from beasts and freezing cold. Cro-Magnon people were hunters. They couldn't exist without animals and perhaps that's why they painted them. We can't be sure, though, that this was actually the reason. We don't know exactly *why* they painted them and we can only guess *how* they did it.

In 1937, fifty-eight years after Don Marcelino's discovery, another remarkable discovery was made at Lussac-les-Châteaux, France. Workers uncovered some strange stone tablets and archaeologists hurried to the scene.

Further digging turned up a store of prehistoric treasures. There were stone axes and other implements, rocks with inscriptions and carvings, and a curious jar resembling a man in a space helmet. Archaeologists called the jar *The Space Traveler* and the name has stuck.

Some of the stone tablets puzzled the scientists just as much as *The Space Traveler*. They showed men, women, and children dressed almost exactly as people dress today. But how could that be? The tablets were estimated to be somewhere around fifteen thousand years old. Cave dwellers wouldn't know anything about hats, shoes, trousers, and shirts. One archaeologist timidly suggested that whoever inspired *The Space Traveler* had shown the Cro-Magnons a photograph of his wife and children. That's certainly an intriguing possibility and it makes as much sense as any other theory.

Three years after the strange discoveries at Lussac-les-Châteaux, a group of schoolboys slid down a rocky chute into a cavern near Lascaux, France. They slid smack into the most amazing cave paintings ever discovered.

Since Don Marcelino had scrambled into the Altamira cave in 1879, paintings had been found in many more caves. Most of them were in France, Spain, and Italy, but several had been discovered in all the other continents of the world. By far the most sensational find, however, was the cave discovered by the schoolboys near Lascaux.

The Louvre in Paris is generally considered to be the world's

A Lascaux cave painting

finest museum of art. The Lascaux cave has often been referred to as "the Louvre of Primitive Art." "It's almost impossible to believe that men dressed only in skins could have achieved such a high degree of skill and delicacy unless they had many generations of tradition and development behind them," declared one observer. An archaeologist said, "The cave paintings at Lascaux have upset all my ideas concerning prehistoric man. He wasn't a savage at all. He was a sensitive being capable of creating great beauty."

One doesn't have to be an art student or a lover of art to appreciate the beauty of the Lascaux cave paintings. They are all vivid and alive and lovely. There are figures of enormous bulls seventeen feet long. A man with the head of a bird is being crushed by a wounded bison. Ponies gallop gaily across low, rolling hills. A herd of stags with huge antlers is swimming across a river. Woolly mammoths stand majestic and alone. One imaginative prehistoric artist painted a mythical monster with the body of a hippopotamus and a deerlike head with long straight horns.

The Lascaux cave presented scholars with a whole pack of problems. Who taught the Cro-Magnons their techniques? Unless they knew how to build scaffolds, how had they managed to paint the ceilings? A fire wouldn't give enough light to paint by, so how had they illuminated the cave? And what was the significance of a man with a bird's head? Did this suggest flight, or was it merely an artist's whim?

A totally different kind of problem popped up fifteen years after the cave had been discovered. Throngs of visitors came to Lascaux to see the paintings, and the authorities were shocked to see that the artwork was being severely damaged. This was serious. The world's greatest treasure of primitive art was in danger of being lost forever. Scientists learned that the damage was caused by the breath expelled by the visitors and they took immediate action.

The cave was closed to the public in the summer of 1955. The French government was determined to protect their tourist attraction from further damage. Engineers installed machinery to purify the air and keep it at a uniform temperature. It is the same method that is used on submarines. A special system was used to eliminate all harmful gases. The temperature and humidity were regulated by electronic devices. Bronze gates were installed at the entrance to keep out the external atmosphere. Once all these protective measures had been taken, visitors were again allowed in to admire the paintings.

MYSTERIES OF
THE EAST AND AFRICA

Baalbek lies northeast of Beirut, Lebanon, at an elevation of thirty-five hundred feet. There are few mysteries on earth that are more intriguing than Baalbek. Nobody knows who built this colossal structure. Neither do they know when it was built or why it was never finished. The workers apparently walked off the job one day and never returned.

"What do you suppose happened to them?" I asked a friend who accompanied me on my first visit to Baalbek.

"Who knows?" My companion shrugged his shoulders. "Maybe they all got into a spaceship and blasted off to some other planet."

I'm not sure that my friend was being entirely serious, but some people believe that this is precisely what did happen. Their reasoning goes something like this: Modern scientists could not build anything like Baalbek, so people living many centuries before the time of Christ certainly couldn't have done it either. If Baalbek couldn't have been built by inhabitants of this world, then it must have been built by beings from another world.

The ruins of Baalbek in Lebanon

Mikhail Agrest, a Russian scientist, agrees. He says that beings from outer space must have built Baalbek, because there has never been a civilization on earth capable of building such a place. He believes, too, that the enormous stone platform upon which the Romans later built the Great Temple was actually a launching pad for space vehicles.

The stone platform at Baalbek is an engineering marvel that could not be duplicated today. Mark Twain, author of *Tom Sawyer* and *Huckleberry Finn,* wrote that "this massive structure might almost support a whole world." And it certainly does look that way. One stretch of the platform is nearly two hundred feet long and is made up of only three stones. Two of them have a length of sixty-four feet each and the third is sixty-nine feet long. These enormous stones were not only cut from the quarry and hewn into shape, but transported to the building site and then somehow hoisted into place, twenty feet above the ground.

The largest cut stone in the world lies in a quarry about half a mile downhill from Baalbek. For some strange reason, it's known as "the Pregnant Stone" and sometimes as "the Stone of the Pregnant Woman," but no one in the Lebanon Tourist and Information Office could tell me why. Neither could the official guide at the ruins.

There's no need to rush to Lebanon to see this enormous stone. It has been lying at the edge of the quarry for thousands of years and it will stay there until someone figures out a way to move it.

This might not be for quite some time yet. The stone is still lying exactly where it was when the unknown builders of Baalbek stopped work. After cutting it out of the cliff and hewing it into the desired shape, they moved it to the edge of the quarry. Then something happened! The workers laid down their tools and never picked them up again. Baalbek was never finished, but the giant stone left behind by the builders is a silent tribute to their genius.

The stone's proportions are staggering. It is fourteen feet thick, seventeen feet wide and seventy feet long. Scholars have estimated its weight at approximately four million pounds.

If the Pregnant Stone was to be used in the construction of Baalbek, this means that the builders knew that they would be able to get it up the hill and lift it into place. They had already done the same thing with stones that were nearly as large and they knew that they could do it with this one.

But how? How could they possibly move a stone that weighed as much as four hundred full-grown bull elephants? Engineers say that there isn't a crane on earth large enough or powerful enough to pick up a four-million-pound load. The ancient builders of Baalbek could do it, though, but we don't know how. They carried their secret away with them and we don't know where they went.

THE INCREDIBLE MAPS OF PIRI REIS

In 1929, some remarkable maps were found in the Topkapi Palace in Istanbul, Turkey. They had been reproduced in 1513 by Piri Reis, a Turkish admiral. A statement on the bottom said that he had copied them from ancient maps he had seen in Egypt.

The maps were sent to the U.S. Navy Hydrographic Bureau for examination. Cartographers studied them carefully, but they couldn't really believe what they were seeing. Everything was fantastically accurate. All of the continents had been drawn in correctly, and even the topography of the interior was shown. Mountain ranges in the Antarctic that had not been discovered until 1952 appeared on the ancient maps of Piri Reis. They were not covered in ice, however, so the scientists concluded that the maps showed the earth's surface as it must have appeared about ten thousand years ago.

This was amazing enough, but the scientists had another big surprise in store for them. The Piri Reis maps bore an uncomfortable similarity to the modern aerial photographs taken by satellites. The confused cartographers searched in vain for some kind of logical explanation. How could this possibly be true? they wondered. Coincidence had to be ruled out. They had the factual evidence in front of them. Someone long before the dawn of recorded history had made accurate maps of our earth.

Scientists who studied the ancient maps at a conference during the International Geophysical Year in 1957 were not able to come up with any answers. Although they agreed that the Piri Reis maps resembled aerial photographs, they couldn't even guess how they had been made. They expressed surprise at their accuracy and detail and had to let it go at that. Being practical and hardheaded scientists, they were understandably reluctant to suggest that the earth might possibly have been photographed from space long before the time of Christ. Any such suggestion would have made them appear ridiculous.

There is no proof that there were any satellites flying around before the twentieth century. Airplanes and spacecraft are still relatively recent inventions. Aerial photography is a modern science and requires very sophisticated camera equipment. As far as we know, early humans could not possibly have taken photographs from any kind of a space vehicle, since the technology for doing so hadn't been developed.

Scientists tell us that early humans lived in caves and dressed in skins and furs. Life was a constant struggle and most of their time was spent hunting and gathering food. Reading and writing were unknown. All they really needed was enough food to eat and enough wood for their fires. Building a spaceship and taking aerial photographs of the earth would have been impossible.

The Topkapi maps became a rather embarrassing issue. They really had no right to exist at all, yet there they were. Somehow or other, before the modern era, human beings had highly accurate maps of our globe. Where did the maps come from? The question intrigued and plagued the scientists.

There seemed to be only one small hint. Piri Reis had copied his maps from the copies of other maps which he had seen in Egypt in 1513. An Egyptian legend handed down through the generations said that a god who came from the skies had given the original maps to a high priest. The maps had been carefully looked after, so the priest must have recognized their value.

We don't know who the god from the skies was and we don't know how the maps were made. Neither do we know why they were given to an Egyptian high priest. Most legends, however, are founded on facts. Although a very highly advanced civilization flourished in the Nile Valley, the Egyptians certainly weren't taking aerial photographs from spaceships ten thousand years ago. We can be very sure of that. And so the mystery of the maps of Piri Reis remains unsolved.

THE VISIONS OF EZEKIEL

Ancient civilizations in all parts of the world had legends about beings from the skies who had lived among them. Paintings and carvings that some people believe are of space travelers and space vehicles have been found in the Americas, Australia, Africa, Europe, and many islands. An increasingly large number of writers and scholars are absolutely convinced that beings from outer space have visited our earth on numerous occasions.

The visions of the prophet Ezekiel puzzled Bible scholars for years. People who believe that the earth has been visited by space travelers believe that Ezekiel's visions are descriptions of space people and space flight vehicles. Ezekiel, of course, believed his visions to be a form of contact with God.

In 1974, a scientist took a hard look at the Book of the Prophet Ezekiel and claimed that he understood what the prophet was saying. Joseph Blumrich is chief of the systems layout branch of the National Aeronautical and Space Administration in Huntsville, Alabama. He has been in aircraft and aerospace engineering for over forty years.

Blumrich readily admits that he only recently began to believe that beings from outer space had visited our earth. It was the accounts written by Ezekiel that first convinced him. Blumrich made detailed drawings based on Ezekiel's descriptions. According to the scientist, the prophet had seen spaceships far in advance of anything we have today, although aerospace engineers have actually had similar futuristic space vehicles on their drawing boards. "The main features of the spaceships described by Ezekiel," says Blumrich, "reveal to us vehicles of surprisingly sophisticated design."

Ezekiel's reports are unique in a number of respects. He says that his visitors actually took him for a ride in some kind of flying machine. They also visited him on several different occasions. Unfortunately, he doesn't tell us how they conversed. Did they use sign language, or did the visitors speak Aramaic? Neither does he tell us how these beings from the skies always managed to find him.

Another curious thing about Ezekiel's experience is that his visitors never stayed around for very long. The majority of legends say that the gods lived with the people on earth and helped them in many ways. They didn't return to their homes until they had taught the people how to live a better life. Ezekiel, too, received a gift. He says he was instructed to prophesy to Israel.

Some legends refer to visitors from the skies as gods, and others refer to them as resembling human beings. Ezekiel says that those who came to see him had "the likeness of a man." And to the prophet they were cherubim and angels. Statues, paintings, and carvings said to be of beings from outer space normally appear more human than godlike.

The idea that our earth has been visited by little green people from Mars is no longer considered seriously by anyone except a few crackpots. None of the legends, in fact, leads us to believe that there was anything strikingly unusual about the beings who came to live with the ancient civilizations. They were often referred to as gods, but that was probably because they came down from the sky, which was believed to be the home of the gods.

If our earth actually has been visited by beings from outer space, then they must have looked very much like the people they came to live with.

Ezekiel's first encounter took place by the Chebar River near Babylon. A mighty wind suddenly came out of the north. A large cloud was inside the wind, and Ezekiel heard "the noise of great waters." There was a "brightness" around the cloud, and fire "flashed forth" continually. In the midst of the cloud, there was something like gleaming metal.

The cloud settled to the ground and "four living creatures" with the "likeness of a man" came out of it. Each of them had four wings and straight legs; their feet were round and sparkled like "burnished brass." The creatures all moved in exactly the same way and at exactly the same time. There was something like "burning coals of fire" amidst them. The fire was bright, and "lightning" shot forth from it.

Spread out over the heads of the living creatures, there was the likeness of a sky. It was shining like rock crystals, and from it came a sound like the "voice of the Almighty." The "likeness of a throne" was above the sky. Something with the appearance of a man was seated upon the throne and there was a "brightness round about" him. Thinking that he was in the presence of the Lord, the prophet fell upon his face. Then a voice called out to Ezekiel, and someone handed him a written scroll, and he was told to go and minister to Israel.

Joseph Blumrich explained the mighty wind, the large cloud, and the noise of the waters. Before the rocket engine could be ignited, his explanation goes, it had to be cooled down to a very low temperature. This was done by forcing liquid hydrogen under pressure from the tank through the cooling system. The hydrogen was later discharged into the atmosphere as a very cold gas. The water in the air froze into ice crystals which formed a large cloud.

The vehicle appears to be inside the cloud and would look like gleaming metal. When the rocket engine was ignited, there would be a brightness surrounding the spaceship and fire flashing from its exhausts.

Joseph Blumrich was almost stumped by Ezekiel's description of four living creatures with wings, straight legs, and round feet that sparkled like burnished brass. While trying to figure this one out, the aerospace engineer remembered an article he had read some years earlier. The article was about a shuttle ship that could travel back and forth between the earth and an orbiting mother ship.

It was the strange design of the shuttle ship that had intrigued Blumrich. It was actually four helicopters fastened together into a single structure. The central body was a pad similar to the lunar-landing module of the Apollo spacecraft. The ship was highly maneuverable and could move slowly back and forth while looking for a place to land.

Blumrich believed that the thing described by Ezekiel was almost exactly the same as the shuttle ship described in the engineering magazine. The four living creatures with the form of human beings who came out of the ship were really the helicopter's landing gears. The four wings were the rotor blades. The straight legs were the landing legs, and the round feet were a type of cushioned footpad that would help the vehicle to land gently and move around without skidding or sliding. Because the four helicopter

Mysteries of the East and Africa

units were joined together, the four living creatures all moved in exactly the same way and at the same time.

Ezekiel then said that there was something like "burning coals of fire" amidst the four living creatures. The fire was bright and "lightning" shot forth from it. This part of the description posed no problem for the aerospace engineer. The glowing radiator of the reactor would have looked like burning coals of fire to the prophet. The lightning that shot forth from it was bursts of flame from the central rockets.

The last part of Ezekiel's description of the space vehicle was by far the easiest for Blumrich to understand. The likeness of a sky spread out over the heads of the living creatures was the command module. It was undoubtedly a strong transparent material, and the desert sunshine made it sparkle like rock crystals. The sound of the "voice of the Almighty" was the roar of the spaceship's engines.

Ezekiel concludes his description by saying that there was the likeness of a throne inside the sky. Something with the appearance of a human was sitting upon the throne and there was a brightness all around it.

Blumrich claims that the throne was the seat of the commander. The prophet had most likely seen only stools and chairs, and the sea with its high back, armrests, and upholstery must have looked like a throne to Ezekiel. What of the form that resembled a human that the prophet believed was God? According to Blumrich, this was the ship's commander dressed in a space suit and helmet.

This, then, is an aerospace engineer's interpretation of Ezekiel's first vision.

BABYLON REDISCOVERED

Some historians tell us that civilization was born about seven thousand years ago on a great plain between the Tigris and Euphrates rivers in the country now known as Iraq. Mighty empires flourished in this region, then decayed and died. There were legends of lovely cities, but all of them had disappeared. Nothing was left on the plain except a few little villages and some enormous mounds.

A number of Europeans had their curiosity aroused by the mounds. Could the lost cities of Assyria and Babylonia be hidden under them they wondered. It seemed reasonable to suppose so. There was little or no stone on the plain. The cities would have been built from bricks fashioned from river mud and dried in the sun. Bricks, of course, would crumble into ruin in time.

One of the first Europeans to investigate the mounds thoroughly was Claudius Rich. He examined one south of Baghdad in 1811 and found bricks with strange inscriptions on them. The inscriptions proved to be cuneiform writing.

Rich became too ill to continue his work, but he published a book on Iraq. He wrote that the whole countryside was covered with ruins. The lost cities of Babylonia and Assyria were buried there, he said, and they were easily accessible to anyone willing to dig for them.

Adventurers, dreamers, and archaeologists hurried to the broad plain between the Tigris and Euphrates. Rich had been right. There were enough mounds for everyone, and some spectacular finds were made almost at once. The strange wedge-shaped writing archaeologists called cuneiform was found everywhere. Many walls covered with sculptures and inscriptions were also discovered and one lucky digger dug up thirteen pairs of huge winged lions.

The excavation of Babylon, the capital of Babylonia, was begun in 1899. Herodotus, a Greek historian, had visited Babylon about 600 B.C. and written that "it surpassed in splendor any city in the known world." He described it in great detail, but the archaeologists believed that he had exaggerated wildly. Herodotus, however, proved to be right.

The city that Herodotus had visited was a brand new one. The old Babylon had been completely destroyed by the Assyrians, a warlike people who lived to the north. King Nebuchadnezzar had rebuilt his capital so that it could withstand any enemy attack.

A wall 80 feet thick, 320 feet high, and thirteen miles long protected the city. The wall was decorated with brightly colored bricks and sculptures of great red and yellow winged lions. A hundred bronze gates were set in this mammoth wall and there were 360

A portion of the towering brick walls of Babylon (in present-day Iraq) built by King Nebuchadnezzar.

watchtowers. A majestic avenue 73 feet wide ran through the heart of the city. It had been built of bricks, then covered with great slabs of white limestone. A double gateway at the end of the avenue was covered by paintings of bulls and dragons.

The ziggurat, a terraced pyramid which may have been the biblical Tower of Babel, was in the most sacred part of the city. It was in a large courtyard surrounded by temples. By far the most impressive temple was the one on the top of the tower. The walls were plated with gold and inlaid with blue enameled bricks. When the sun was shining on the temple, the dazzling light could be seen throughout the city.

The inside of the temple must have been a truly fabulous sight. There was a huge golden statue of the god Marduk, and even the furniture was made of gold. Herodotus wrote that there were twenty-six tons of gold in the temple's interior alone. At today's prices, the gold would be worth approximately $150 million.

Another exciting find was the Hanging Gardens of Babylon, one of the Seven Wonders of the World. King Nebuchadnezzar had built the gardens because his young wife missed the green hills of her native land. Thousands upon thousands of tons of soil were brought to the palace ground. The gardens rose, terrace by terrace, until they were the height of a thirty-story skyscraper. Grass, flowers, and trees were planted, and the young queen had her green hills.

The real wonder of the Hanging Gardens of Babylon was the system used to bring water from the Euphrates River. Archaeologists believe that a series of pumps must have been used, but they're not happy with this thought. Pumping water 350 feet into the air is a complicated procedure and takes sophisticated machinery. Could people who lived six centuries before the time of Christ have been capable of such an accomplishment? they wondered.

The archaeologists aren't sure. The ancient Babylonians were gifted mathematicians, astronomers, and engineers. They accomplished many amazing things and they may even have been able to make water run uphill. More and more examples of the genius of ancient civilizations are coming to light all the time, and the world has become accustomed to amazing discoveries. Just about everyone is now willing to admit that people living thousands of years

Mysteries of the East and Africa 79

before Christ possessed skills that still aren't fully understood today.

THE LOST SUMERIANS

Cuneiform writing was found in many places in Assyria and Babylonia, and quite a few scholars learned how to read it. This led to a startling bit of information. An archaeologist digging near Basra in present-day Iraq uncovered some clay tablets that referred to the king of Sumer.

The king of Sumer? the scholars asked one another. Now who in the world is he? It was an intriguing question that baffled everyone. Nobody had ever heard of him and nobody knew where Sumer was. Neither was anything at all known about the Sumerians.

The story unfolded slowly over the next fifty years. The Sumerian civilization, it was learned, went back as far as 4500 B.C. Cuneiform writing was developed about a thousand years later and detailed records were kept. Thanks to these records and the scholars' ability to read them, we know much about the Sumerians. We do not know, however, where these mysterious people came from. Robert Silverberg, author of *Lost Cities and Vanished Civilizations,* says that they may have come from India, but admits that this is only his opinion.

The Sumerians are said to have been the first human beings to create a true civilization. How they were able to start from scratch and make such a swift and dramatic leap forward is not known. There was nothing to guide them along the path to civilization, because nobody had ever traveled that path before. Erich von Daniken says that they must have been helped along by gods from outer space, and some people are inclined to agree with him.

The Sumerians were a highly intelligent and ambitious people. They lived by farming and fishing and they lived well. Canals and reservoirs were built to irrigate their lands. They used wagons, plows, and sailboats. They had measuring instruments, surveying tools, and the potter's wheel. Copper, bronze, paints, leather, perfumes, drugs, and a host of other things were known to them. Medicine was a well-developed science. There were Sumerian artists, musicians, and poets. There may even have been Sumerian astronauts.

Twelve clay tablets found in the mound of Kuyunjik tell of the adventures of Gilgamesh, a Sumerian hero who was part god and part man. Gilgamesh decided to visit the home of the gods and he asked an eagle to carry him there. Several of the tablets are devoted to the story of his flight through the sky.

This could be dismissed as a fairy tale, of course, but some of the things make one stop and think. Gilgamesh describes his flight in great detail. He tells how the earth and sea looked as he is carried higher and higher. The descriptions are convincingly accurate. From a great height, the land looked like porridge and the sea like a watering trough.

Nobody could ask for a better description. Aerial photographs taken from American spaceships show that the desert regions look more like porridge than anything else. His description of the sea is also excellent. Gilgamesh would have seen either the Red Sea or the Persian Gulf from high in the sky. He said that the sea looked like a watering trough and he's right. Both of these bodies of water are much longer than they are wide and this holds true of a watering trough as well.

We know very well that Gilgamesh wasn't carried through the air by an eagle. We don't know how he was carried, but he must have reached a great height or he couldn't have described the world as he did. Unless, of course, he heard the description from someone else. But whom? A visitor from outer space? Unfortunately, that question is another one that can't be answered. The fact remains, though, that someone looked down on the earth from a very great height and gave an accurate description of what they saw.

Like so many ancient civilizations, the Sumerians were deeply interested in space and flight. Cuneiform tablets told of gods who rode through the skies in fiery ships. Other gods came down from the stars, visited them for a time, and then returned to the stars. Carvings were found in mounds showing people with stars on their heads. There were also carvings of circles with wings and of people traveling among the stars on balls.

It's interesting to note, too, that it was in the land between the Tigris and Euphrates rivers that Ezekiel had his visions. It's possible, then, that the Sumerians were also visited by men from other space, and this might help to explain their tremendous accomplishments.

THE QUEEN OF SHEBA

The Queen of Sheba is probably the most famous queen in history. We are told in the Bible that she came to visit King Solomon in Jerusalem "with a very great train, with camels that bore spices and very much gold and precious stones." The queen's identity, however, is as much of a mystery as the location of King Solomon's mines.

There is a short reference to the queen in the Old Testament, but no other mention of her has ever been found in any language. In spite of this, several stories, novels, and plays have been written about her. Although she has been portrayed in a number of movies, the Bible doesn't tell us what she looked like. The Hollywood version, of course, always pictures her as a very rich and exquisitely beautiful young woman who immediately captures the heart of King Solomon.

But where was the land over which this rich and beautiful queen ruled? That is a question that still puzzles historians and archaeologists. They assume that this land so rich in gold, spices, and precious stones must have been in either Asia or Africa and that's as close as they can get.

Some scholars think that Sheba may have been the ancient Arabian kingdom of Saba which was conquered by the Assyrians. Saba had important ports on the Red Sea and it's probable that ships sailing between India and Egypt stopped there to trade. King Solomon ruled about one thousand years before the time of Christ, and Saba was then a rich and fairly powerful nation.

Extensive ruins and numerous inscriptions discovered in the southwestern part of the Arabian Peninsula prove that the Sabaeans had reached a high level of civilization. Marib, the capital, was in the highlands and it's here that the Queen of Sheba would have had her palace. A palace has been found, but none of the hundreds of inscriptions make any mention of a queen.

This fact doesn't particularly worry those who believe that the Queen of Sheba came from ancient Saba. They say that the queen was merely the king's wife and not the ruler of the kingdom. A reigning monarch, they point out, could not have left her country and gone off to visit King Solomon. It's a journey of fifteen hundred miles from Marib to Jerusalem. The queen made the trip on a camel, so she would have been away from her kingdom for at least several months. A king's wife, on the other hand, could very well have visited Solomon as her husband's ambassador.

The question of the whereabouts of Saba is made more complicated by the existence of another kingdom with the same name. This one lay high in the mountains of Ethiopia. It was about one hundred miles east of Aksum, the capital of a former kingdom once known as the Axumite Empire.

The Ethiopian Saba was an important religious center believed to have been founded by an Arabian culture. It is known that trade was carried on with people on the Arabian Peninsula and almost certainly with Israel, Egypt, and other countries as well. The chief gods of the Sabaeans were the sun, the moon, and the planet Venus.

An Ethiopian legend claims that their kings are direct descendants of Solomon and the Queen of Sheba. According to the legend, a merchant told the queen about the wealth and wisdom of King Solomon. She was so impressed by what she heard that she decided to make the long journey to Jerusalem to see him. Solomon liked the beautiful queen who had traveled so far to visit him and gave her a palace next to his own. A son was born to the queen on her long journey home and she named him Menelik. The little prince was the first of the royal line of Ethiopian kings and emperors.

Until Emperor Haile Selassie was overthrown recently, all of the kings and emperors of Ethiopia had been known as the Elect of God and the Lion of Judah. The Queen of Sheba was the mother of the country and King Solomon was the father.

There is, of course, no solid evidence that this legend is founded on fact. The whereabouts of the land rich in gold, spices, and precious stones which was ruled over by the mysterious and

Mysteries of the East and Africa

beautiful Queen of Sheba is still unknown and it may remain lost forever. The Bible tells us very little about the queen and nothing at all about her country.

ZIMBABWE—AN AFRICAN RIDDLE

In 1868, a South African named Adam Renders discovered the ruins of Zimbabwe in the wild and savagely beautiful bush country of southern Rhodesia. Renders was hunting elephants in virtually unexplored territory when he suddenly came across a curious complex of buildings. There were high circular towers, stone monuments, and a fortresslike structure surrounded by a massive wall topped by turrets.

Renders must have been an extremely unimaginative man. The ruins scarcely aroused his curiosity. He had a quick look around to see if he could find any hidden treasure, then he continued on his way. He never returned to Zimbabwe, but he mentioned casually to his friends that he had found the ruins of an old city or something out in the bush. Then he'd add that there wasn't any treasure or anything else of interest in the place.

Nobody got excited about Zimbabwe until Karl Mauch, a German scientist, visited it in 1871. Mauch had a knowledge of geology and he believed that there were rich deposits of gold nearby. He even discovered the remains of mines that had been worked by unknown miners long, long ago.

Mauch made a detailed study of the ruins, then announced his belief that Zimbabwe was the remains of a fortress of Ophir. The Old Testament says that Ophir was a region where much gold was found and Mauch took things a step further. Ophir, he said, was a wild country which had been governed about 1000 B.C. by a vassal of the Queen of Sheba. The German believed that the mines of King Solomon had been in Ophir and many scholars agreed with him.

Some archaeologists, however, have different opinions. Richard Hall and other British scholars say it's more likely that Zimbabwe was a Phoenician mining center. Others think that Zimbabwe was built by the Egyptians, and still others think it was the Minoans or

The Zimbabwe ruins of Rhodesia

some lost civilization from North Africa or the Arabian Peninsula who built it. Still other scholars say Zimbabwe is a Bantu structure of medieval origin, at the earliest.

Archaeologists have had a tough time of it at Zimbabwe because there are no inscriptions to guide them and many things to confuse them. There is a temple, but nobody has yet learned which god was worshiped by the unknown builders. The design of the temple and the design of the fortress are unlike anything ever built by any known civilization.

Although it has been pretty well established that the people of Zimbabwe were in contact with people from other parts of the world, this only adds to the mystery. Pearls and gold bracelets believed to be from the Arabian Peninsula have been found near the ruins, and so have art objects said to have originated in India. Carvings of animals on a stone monument near the temple remind some archaeologists of animal carvings they have seen in India and North America. Most confusing of all is the bird carved on top of a pillar. This could be the mythical thunderbird of the North American Indians or the mythical phoenix of the Egyptians, or it could be something entirely different. Nobody knows, but the Republic of Rhodesia has taken the strange bird as its national emblem.

Perhaps nothing at Zimbabwe—except Zimbabwe itself—has aroused as much controversy as the towers. We can't imagine what purpose they were supposed to serve, but Robert Charroux makes an interesting observation.

> We find at Zimbabwe, as at Machu Picchu in Peru, high oval towers like silos with no openings in their walls as though they could only be inhabited by winged beings. At Machu Picchu they are in fact called the abodes of winged men. We believe that these were human beings who possessed the secret of movement through space, as tradition attests in America, Asia and Africa. It may be, then, that Zimbabwe and Machu Picchu were both inhabited by a race of mankind endowed with knowledge which is a sealed book to us.

We don't know why winged beings would want to be cooped up inside a tower. Neither do we know why the towers were built nor who built them. Everything about this strange ruin in the lonely, lovely African bush is shrouded in mystery. We know very little more about it now than was known a few years after its discovery.

Until the puzzle of Zimbabwe has been solved, we can accept the theory we like best. We can believe that Zimbabwe was inhabited by winged beings, or that it was a fortress built to guard the mines of King Solomon, or that it was once a part of the realm of the Queen of Sheba.

If none of these theories about Zimbabwe appeal to us, there are plenty more to choose from.

THE FLYING MACHINES OF INDIA

The literature of ancient India frequently mentions flying machines capable of traveling great distances. They were called *vimanas* and were far more sophisticated than anything we have today.

A Sanskrit manuscript believed to be five thousand years old describes the construction and use of *vimanas*. This information was condensed into a series of articles entitled "Aircraft of the Prehistoric Past" and was published in a popular Indian magazine. Although the central theme of the manuscript was easily understood, translators had difficulty with the technical portions. Thirty-one pieces of machinery were described in great detail, but there was some doubt about their exact function. The metals also presented a problem because the translators could only identify three of the sixteen listed as necessary for the construction.

The *vimanas,* we are told, could fly from country to country and from world to world. They flew so high and so fast that they couldn't be seen from the ground. They had long, tapered shapes and no wings. Their main source of energy was heated mercury, and the *vimanas* always blasted off with a big roar and a stream of fire. Once the spaceship had attained sufficient altitude, it could keep going round and round the world for an indefinite period of time as our satellites do in the twentieth century. The description actually sounds very much like that of a rocket being launched at Cape Kennedy.

The course of enemy flying machines could be followed by some undisclosed means. Pictures could be taken of the interiors of enemy aircraft, and the conversations of the crews could be overheard. Enemy *vimanas* could either be destroyed from the ground or captured by making the crews unconscious. It was also possible to bring an enemy spaceship to a complete stop.

We aren't told whether the *vimanas* were built in India or whether they came from another world. It seems, though, that visitors from space visited the ancient Indians quite regularly. Scholars say that there are several hundred stories telling about visits from gods. Many Indians insist that the Sanskrit texts have some basis of truth. They are firmly convinced that their ancestors were in contact with people who came from the skies.

It would be interesting to know why so much of a Sanskrit manuscript was devoted to the construction and use of *vimanas*. Did one of the gods dictate the directions so that humans could build their own spaceship? Was the manuscript perhaps a textbook

Mysteries of the East and Africa

for astronauts and engineers? Was it written by someone from this world or by someone from another planet?

Unfortunately, we don't know. We don't know, either, whether a spaceship could be built by following the directions exactly. Some parts of the text are not yet understood, but scholars at India's Mysore International Academy of Sanskrit Studies are still working on the translations. According to a member of the academy, "The manuscripts describe various types of automatic ships adapted for travel in air and from planet to planet. It seems that they could stop still in the sky and even become invisible; and that they might have instruments capable of detecting hostile aircraft at a distance."

A number of manuscripts tell about terrible weapons carried by the *vimanas*. From their descriptions, the prehistoric authors could have been speaking of poison gas, napalm bombs, and nuclear bombs. One weapon was capable of producing a fire that would reduce the army of an enemy to ashes. Another one would put their enemies to sleep, and still another would attack the nervous system of their enemies and make them powerless.

Here is the description of a superbomb taken from the translation of a Sanskrit manuscript.

> They launched a huge missile of burning fire and thick darkness fell upon the armies and on everything. A terrible wind arose and blood-colored clouds swept down onto the earth. The enemy fell like shrubs consumed by the fire. The rivers boiled and those who jumped into them perished miserably. The forests burned; horses and elephants plunged wildly through them, neighing and trumpeting. When the wind had cleared away the smoke, we beheld thousands of corpses burned to ashes.

This must have been a terrible weapon, but one even more deadly is described in a translation of the *Mahabharata*. Parts of the text are quoted by Erich von Daniken in *Chariots of the Gods* and by Peter Kolosimo in *Timeless Earth*. It says:

> The god, flying in a *vimana* of great power, dropped on the city a missile weighted with all the force of the universe. An incandescent smoke, brighter than ten thousand suns, rose in all its splendor. It was an unknown weapon, a gigantic messenger of death that burnt to

ashes all the inhabitants. It was as if all the elements had been released. Scorched by the heat of the weapon, the world reeled in fever. Elephants were set on fire and sank dead to the ground. The water boiled and the raging of the blaze made the trees collapse in rows. Horses and chariots were burnt up over a vast area. Then a deep silence descended. The winds began to blow and the earth grew bright. It was a terrible sight to see. The corpses of the fallen were mutilated by the terrible heat so that they no longer looked like human beings. Never before have we seen such a ghastly weapon and never before have we heard of such a weapon.

This is truly an incredible description. A flying machine drops a missile on a city. The explosion that follows is brighter than ten thousand suns. People, elephants, horses, and chariots are burned to ashes. Water boils and trees collapse in rows. Then a deep silence descends.

It sounds as if the writer is describing a plane dropping a nuclear bomb. But how could that be? The *Mahabharata* was written about five thousand years ago.

That leaves us with two unanswered questions: Did the ancient writer have a very vivid imagination which was let run wild? Or did a flying machine in ages past actually drop a missile that killed every living thing in a city? A prehistoric bombing may sound utterly fantastic, but there might be some evidence that such an event really did take place.

Indian archaeologists excavating the ruins of a Buddhist temple in 1947 came upon the remains of an ancient city which they called Mohenjo-Daro. Although it was impossible to learn who had built the city and who had lived there, it was obvious that the inhabitants had attained a high degree of civilization. The main street was thirty-three feet wide and over half a mile long. All of the houses were expertly built of fire-baked bricks. There was running water and a bathroom in every house. Pipes and drains under the streets carried all the waste to the Indus River. British engineers who visisted Mohenjo-Daro declared that the plumbing system could only have been designed by skilled and well-trained technicians.

The unknown people of Mohenjo-Daro must have lived well. Jewels, rings, bracelets, and necklaces of gold, silver, and ivory were found in many houses. The children played with an inter-

An ancient miniature from India showing women dancing with sky gods. India's earliest mythology tells of gods who traveled the air in luminous cars.

esting assortment of toys. They even had a heated swimming pool to splash around in.

There was always enough food to feed everyone. The Indus River was full of fish. Rice and wheat were planted in fields near the city. Cattle, sheep, and water buffalo grazed on the riverbank. Plenty of edible roots, berries, and fruit could be found in the forests. Elephants were used as beasts of burden and perhaps also as food.

Life in Mohenjo-Daro ended about four thousand years ago. The inhabitants simply vanished without a trace. They were there one minute and gone the next. It looked as though they had just walked out of their houses and never returned. There was no sign of panic or haste. Everything was left in good order.

A hint of what might have happened finally came to light. A fire of intense heat had swept through the city. It hadn't been an ordinary fire, however, because the brick houses would have been poor fuel. The fire had exploded all at once. Leaping flames of raging heat had suddenly engulfed everyone. There was no escape for the unfortunate inhabitants, and all of them died in the fiery furnace of Mohenjo-Daro.

Every educated Indian is familiar with the *Mahabharata* and the archaeologists remembered reading about "an unknown weapon, a gigantic messenger of death that burnt to ashes all the inhabitants." Is that what happened at Mohenjo-Daro? they asked one another. Had all the people been burned to ashes, then blown away by the wind? No signs of human remains had been found, so it certainly seemed possible.

Peter Kolosimo says, "Science has no answer to the mystery of Mohenjo-Daro, but some scientists believe that the answer is obvious: men, women and children were 'atomized' by some terrible means of disintegration. This may seem far-fetched, yet who can say that it's not true?"

THE ASTRONAUT OF THE SAHARA DESERT

Although the Lascaux cave paintings are undoubtedly the most beautiful, those found in the Tassili-n-Ajjer region in the Algerian Sahara are the most unusual. There are thousands of figures of hu-

Tassili paintings discovered by Henri Lhote in the Sahara.

mans and animals and it seems that an entire school of artists was at work there.

The strangest painting of them all has been called *The Great God of the Martians* by Henri Lhote, the French explorer who discovered the caves. The figure is over eighteen feet high. It's rather crudely done, but the man appears to be wearing a space suit. The helmet is round and there are holes for the eyes and a slit for the mouth. There are antennae on the helmet, and the man seems to be floating in space. A photograph of this figure appeared in many newspapers beside a photograph of Yuri Gagarin, Russia's first astronaut.

One scene shows something resembling a flying saucer with the hatch open. Five giant figures nearly twelve feet tall are floating in the air beside it. All of them are wearing tight-fitting white helmets with red dots. It's the sort of picture a child might draw of astronauts landing on a planet in outer space.

Giants as well as astronauts figured strongly in the paintings of prehistoric Tassili artists. Many of the figures are from ten to twelve feet high. Men of normal height seem to be servants of the giants or perhaps are worshiping them as gods. The Watusis of central Africa are reputedly the tallest people in the world and it's possible that there was some form of contact between the two races.

There are also a great number of paintings of gazelles, giraffes, zebras, lions, elephants, and other African animals. These, however, can be explained easily. The pictures were painted around 8000 B.C. and at that time the area was not a desert. It was a wooded area with great rivers. The population was fairly dense, and great herds of wild animals lived in the forests. Then the climate became hotter and hotter. The rivers dried up; the forests withered and died. Little food could be found in the sandy wastes, and the people and animals were forced to move south.

Except for the fact that they left thousands of curious paintings behind them, we know nothing at all about the people who were driven south by the encroaching sands of the Sahara Desert.

THE GODS

There are billions of stars in our Milky Way and most of these stars have planets. A growing number of scientists now agree that many of these planets are able to support life. Many of them may even support civilizations vastly more intelligent than our own.

Dr. Carl Sagan, a world-famous scientist, estimates that there are at least fifty thousand civilizations in our galaxy alone. Some of them may have attained a very high degree of technological knowledge. "It's quite likely," says Dr. Sagan, "that astronauts from these distant planets have visited Earth in ages past. Thousands of these planets are almost exact duplicates of Earth and visiting astronauts would have felt quite at home. Their appearances, too, must have been very similar to that of people here on Earth."

The histories of many ancient civilizations follow a fairly fixed pattern. Stone Age hunters and food gatherers became skilled artisans in an incredibly short time. Their great leap forward was nothing short of miraculous. People of nomadic tribes became citizens of powerful empires almost overnight. Fabulous cities sprang up on sky-scraping plateaus, on bleak plains, and in river valleys. Temples, pyramids, bridges, and roads were built. Astronomy, engineering, and mathematics became exact sciences. Virtually all of the prehistoric societies developed a written language.

Very few of these ancient civilizations claim to have made such dramatic progress entirely on their own. In most cases, credit has been given to the gods. The gods lived with the people for a time, then went back to where they had come from. A number of them, however, promised to return and this promise sometimes caused dreadful suffering. One reason for the tragic end of the Aztec, Maya, and Inca civilizations was the belief that the plundering Spaniards were the bearded gods who legend said had once lived with them and helped them in so many ways.

The advance of certain early civilizations followed curious courses which still aren't understood by us today. The Easter Islanders devoted all their time and energy to carving huge stone statues. Unknown artisans created Tiahuanaco with its massive mysterious Gate of the Sun. The Mayas were dedicated to the study of time and astronomy. Fortresses, temples, and a swift means of communication seem to have been the chief interests of the Incas. The Aztecs and Egyptians erected colossal pyramids. Prehistoric artists painted strikingly lovely paintings in caves in Spain, France, Italy, and the Sahara Desert. Gigantic figures which can only be properly appreciated when seen from the air are found in Europe and in both North and South America. The Sumerians, Khmers, Aztecs, Incas, and other cultures built magnificent cities. The ancient Indians were talented mathematicians, and their craftspeople could do things with certain metals that still aren't understood at this time.

Very few things have puzzled archaeologists more than the gigantic stone structures that were erected before or soon after the dawn of history. These massive creations are found on South Pacific islands, high in the South American Andes, deep in Central American jungles, on the rolling plains of France and England, along the banks of the Nile, and in a number of other locations. The sad fact is that we know so very little about most of these giant stone creations. We can't be sure exactly why they were built or how they were built. Neither do we know why so many civilizations living thousands of miles apart shared certain secrets of working with stone.

The Gods

Engineers today admit that they could not build a Tiahuanaco, a Baalbek, or a Great Pyramid. How, then, were the ancients able to do it? Were they taught by the gods?

Scientists are practical people. Although the thought is a terrifying one, they are aware of the fact that civilization as we know it now may someday cease to exist. American cities could be wiped out by warfare. Intense radioactivity could turn the United States into a wasteland. All traces of our civilization could disappear from the face of the earth. Visitors from outer space or other continents might not even realize that they were standing on the site of what was once the world's richest and most powerful nation.

Americans, of course, hope and pray that such a thing will never happen. They know, though, that no civilization has lasted forever. Many have simply disappeared without a trace. To keep that from happening to our country, scientists decided to leave a memento of our civilization that will last for thousands of years. The memento was more than just a written record of our history and accomplishments. It also contained an assortment of items that are familiar to most people today.

The memento was the idea of people working for Westinghouse Electric Company. The World's Fair was held in New York in 1939 and 1940 and the memento was a part of the Westinghouse exhibit. All the objects were packed into a "Time Capsule" and the capsule was addressed to the people of A.D. 6939. This date was exactly 5,000 years after the opening date of the New York World's Fair.

Workers on the Westinghouse site dug a hole fifty feet deep and lined it with double steel tubing. The bottom was sealed with sand and concrete. The capsule was a cartridge seven and a half feet long. It was made of Westinghouse nickel and silver-alloy copper and lined with Pyrex glass.

An interesting assortment of items was packed into the tube: a woman's hat, razor, can opener, fountain pen, pencil, tobacco pouch with zipper, pipe, tobacco, cigarettes, camera, eyeglasses, toothbrush, cosmetics, textiles, metals and alloys, coal, building materials, synthetic plastics, seeds, dictionaries, language texts, magazines, and written records on microfilm. The tube was then emptied of air, filled with inert nitrogen, and hermetically sealed.

In order to make reasonably sure that archaeologists in 6939 would know about the capsule, Westinghouse sent books of records to all the world's leading libraries. The books told them how to calculate the date when the capsule should be opened. The dates of the Gregorian, Chinese, Mohammedan, and Jewish calendars were also included—and the astronomical time, in case no calendars existed at that period.

The exact latitude and longitude of the capsule's well were calculated to less than an inch. There was a possibility that these figures might be slightly off thousands of years later because of continental drift, so directions were included for locating the capsule with electromagnetic instruments.

On 27 September 1940, a large crowd gathered at Westinghouse's World Fair site on Long Island. A huge cauldron containing five hundred pounds of hot petroleum pitch was poured into the well. Chlorinated biphenyl and mineral oil had been added to the pitch to make it resistant to moisture and soil acids.

The well was sealed at the stroke of noon. Spectators solemnly bowed their heads. A bugle sounded taps. The capsule started on its long journey through time.

People living today will never know the fate of the Westinghouse Time Capsule buried on Long Island. It's most reasonable to suppose, though, that other capsules were buried thousands of years ago by other advanced civilizations. Perhaps their locations were given in the books and papyruses destroyed by misguided persons. Perhaps some still lie hidden in the ruins of buried cities.

If any are ever found, we will know a great deal more about the unknown gods and beings who may have visited earth in ages past.

BIBLIOGRAPHY

Allen, Percy. *The Calendar of Tiahuanaco*. London: Faber & Faber, 1956.
Bellamy, Hans. *Built before the Flood*. London: Faber & Faber, 1943.
Berlitz, Charles. *Mysteries from Forgotten Worlds*. London: Souvenir Press, 1972.
Blumrich, J. F. *The Spaceships of Ezekiel*. New York: Bantam, 1974.
Bord, Janet and Colin. *Mysterious Britain*. London: Garnstone Press, 1972.
Ceram, C. W. *Gods, Graves and Scholars*. London: Sidgwick & Jackson, 1952.
Charroux, Robert. *Forgotten Worlds*. London: Souvenir Press, 1972.
———. *Lost Worlds: Scientific Secrets of the Ancients*. London: Souvenir Press, 1974.
Coe, Michael D. *The Maya*. London: Penguin Books, 1971.
De Camp, L. Sprague and Catherine C. *Citadels of Mystery*. London: Souvenir Press, 1965.
Drake, Raymond W. *Gods and Spacemen in the Ancient West*. London: Sphere Books, 1974.
Dutt, Romesh. *The Ramayana and the Mahabharata*. London: Dent, 1961.
Edwards, Frank. *The Pyramids of Egypt*. London: Max Parrish, 1961.
———. *Stranger Than Science*. London: Pan Books, 1963.
Fairservis, Walter A. *The Ancient Kingdoms of the Nile*. New York: New American Library, 1962.
Fort, Charles. *New Lands*. New York: Ace Books, 1973.
Hawkins, Gerald S. *Stonehenge Decoded*. London: Souvenir Press, 1966.
Heyerdahl, Thor. *Aku-Aku*. New York: Pocket Books, 1958.
Homet, Marcel. *On the Trail of the Sun Gods*. London: Neville Spearman, 1965.
Howard, Cecil, and Parry, J. H. *Pizarro and the Conquest of Peru*. New York: Harper and Row, 1968.

Hyne, C. J. Cutliffe. *The Lost Continent*. London: Pan Books, 1974.
Irwin, Constance. *Fair Gods and Stone Faces*. London: W. H. Allen, 1963.
Kolosimo, Peter. *Not of This Earth*. London: Souvenir Press, 1970.
———. *Timeless Earth*. London: Sphere Books, 1974.
Landsburg, Alan and Sally. *In Search of Ancient Mysteries*. New York: Bantam, 1974.
Maringer, Johannes. *The Gods of Prehistoric Man*. London: Weidenfeld & Nicholson, 1960.
Mason, J. A. *The Ancient Civilizations of Peru*. rev. ed. New York: Penguin, 1969.
Silverberg, Robert. *Lost Cities and Vanished Civilizations*. New York: Bantam, 1974.
Toffler, Alvin. *Future Shock*. New York: Bantam, 1971.
Tomas, Andrew. *We Are Not the First*. New York: Bantam, 1973.
Von Hagen, Victor W. *Aztec: Man and Tribe*. London: New English Library, 1960.
Wellard, James. *The Search for Lost Worlds*. London: Pan Books, 1975.
Williamson, George Hunt. *Secret Places of the Lion*. London: Futura Publications, 1974.

INDEX

Adena mound, *illus.*, 45
Africa, antiquities in, 83–85
Agrest, Mikhail, 69
Aircraft, ancient, 85–90
Airfields, ancient, 2–3, 5–6, 48
Aksum, 82
Algeria, antiquities in, 90–92
Allen, Percy, *The Calendar of Tiahuanaco*, 10
Altamira cave paintings (Spain), 59–62
America, discovery of, 49–50
Andes, Candelabra of, 3, 9
Assawompset Pond, Mass., 50
Assyria, 76, 79
Astronomy, ancient, 2, 44, 53–54
Atahualpa, 12

Atlantis, 34, 42
Avebury (England), 56–57
Axumite Empire, 82
Aztec Calendar Stone, *illus.*, 35
Aztecs, 33–36, 40

Baalbek, 67–70
Babel, Tower of, 78
Babylon, 73, 75–79
Basra, 79
Bay of Pisco, 3
Beirut, 67
Bellamy, Hans, *Built before the Flood*, 10
Berlitz, Charles, 37, 43
Mysteries from Forgotten Worlds, 49

Bible, 72–75, 78, 81, 83
Bingham, Hiram, 17
Bird Mound (Wisconsin), 44
Blumrich, Joseph, 72–75
Bolivia, antiquities in, 7–11
Bonampak, 42
Bounaud, Humberto, 5–7

Cahokia (Illinois), 46
Cajamarca (Peru), 12
Caldera, Salvador, 4
Calendars, ancient, 2, 8–10; *illus.,* 35
California, antiquities in, 46–47
Camels, 4
Candelabra of the Andes, 3, 9
Cartography, ancient, 70–71
Caso, Dr. Alfonso, 39
Cataclysmic upheavals, 11
Catherwood, Frederick, 41
Cave paintings, 59–64, 90–92
Central America, antiquities in, 33–44
Cerne Abbas Giant (Dorset), 48
Charlottesville, Va., mound near, 44
Charroux, Robert, 2, 9, 85
Chebar River, 73
Chichén Itzá, 41–42
Chile, desert drawings and carvings in, 4–7
Cholula, 40
Coe, Dr. Michael D., *The Maya,* 41

Colombia, shell mounds in, 45
Congress of Prehistorians, 60
Conquistadores, 11–12, 33–35, 40–41
Copán ruins, 42; *illus.,* 6
Cortes, Hernando, 33–34, 40
Cuneiform writing, 76, 79–80
Cuzco, 14–16

Dancers' Gallery (Monte Albán), 38–40, 43
Daniken, Erich von, 2, 28–29, 43, 48
Chariots of the Gods, 87
Death Valley (California), 47
DeCamp, L. Sprague, *Citadels of Mystery,* 26–27
Doheny Expedition, 1923, 48
Drake, W. Raymond, 34, 38, 43
Gods and Spacemen in the Ancient West, 43, 48

Eagle Mound (Georgia), 44
Easter Island, 20–29; *illus.,* 22, 25
Edwards, Frank, *Stranger than Science,* 48
Egypt, 71
El Enladrillado plateau, 5–7
England, antiquities in, 53–59
Ethiopia, 82
Euphrates River, 75, 78
Eyraud, Brother Eugène, 23–24
Ezekiel, 72–75, 80

Index

Fawcett, Col. P. H., 20
France, antiquities in, 62–64

Gate of the Sun (Tiahuanaco), 8–10
Giant Hill (Dorset), 58
Gilgamesh, 80
Gog Magog Giants (Cambridge), 58–59
Gordon, Dr. Cyrus, 50
Grand Canyon, 48
Gravity, laws of, 18–20, 28
Great Britain, antiquities in, 53–59
Great Serpent Mound (Ohio), *illus.*, 45

Haile Selassie, Emperor, 82
Hall, Richard, 83
Hanging Gardens of Babylon, 78
Hawkins, Dr. Gerald S., 54–55, 57
  Stonehenge Decoded, 53
Herodotus, 76, 78
Heyerdahl, Thor, 21, 23–24, 26–27
Homet, Marcel, 34
Honduras, ruins in, *illus.*, 6
Horbiger, Hans, 10–11

Ice Age, 62
Icknield Ridgeway (England), 57

Inca Empire, 11–20
India, antiquities in, 85–90
International Geophysical Year, 1957, 70
Inyo County, Calif., 47
Irwin, Constance, *Fair Gods and Stone Faces,* 34

Jefferson, Thomas, 44

Kazantsev, Alexander, 9, 11
Kolosimo, Peter, 4, 43, 90
  Timeless Earth, 87
Kon-Tiki, 21
Kosok, Dr. Paul, 1–2
Kukulcán, 41
Kuyunjik (Iraq), 80

Lake Titicaca, 7, 11
Landsbury, Alan, 2, 43, 48
Lascaux cave paintings (France), 62–64, 90
Lethbridge, T. C., 58
Lhote, Henri, 92
Long Man of Wilmington (Sussex), 58
Lussac-les-Chateaux cave paintings (France), 62–64

Machu Picchu, 17–20, 85
Mahabharata, 87–88, 90
Maps, ancient, 70–71
Marcahuasi, 3, 9

Marduk, 78
Marib, 81
Mauch, Karl, 83
Mayas, 41–44
Mechanicsburg, Penn., 49
Menelik, 82
Mexico, antiquities in, 33–40
Middle East, antiquities in, 67–83
Minoan civilization, 50
Mohenjo-Daro (India), 88–90
Mojave Maze (California), 46–47
Monk's Mound (Illinois), 46
Monte Albán (Mexico), excavations in, 38–40, 43
Montezuma, 33–34, 40
Morgantown, Tenn., 49
Mounds and mound builders, North American, 44–46. *See also* Stonehenge mounds; Silbury Hill.
Mystery Hill (New Hampshire), 49

Nazca desert, 1–3, 9
Nebuchadnezzar, King, 76
North America, antiquities in, 44–50

Oaxaca, 38–40, 43
Olav V, King of Norway, 21
Olmecs, 36–40
Ophir, 83
Outer space, visitors from, to ancient civilizations, 2, 4–5, 9, 28, 43, 72–75, 80–81, 95–96

Pacific, ancient civilizations in, 20–29
Palenque, 42–43
Pattee, Jonathan, 49
Peru
  Ancient drawings and carvings in, 1–5
  Inca Empire, 11–20
  relations with Easter Island natives, 28
Phoenicians, 49–50
Piri Reis, 70–71
Pisco, Bay of, 3
Pitcairn Island, 23
Pizarro, Francisco, 11–13, 33
Posnanski, Dr. Arturo, 8, 10, 11
"Pregnant Stone" (Lebanon), 69
Prescott, W. H., 40
  History of the Conquest of Peru, 14

Queen of Sheba, 81–83
Quetzalcoatl, 33–34, 40–41
Quipu, 16–17

Reiche, Dr. Maria, 2–3
  Secret of the Desert, 3
Renders, Adam, 83

Index

Rhodesia, antiquities in, 83–85
Rich, Claudius, 76
Robot, drawing of, 4–5
Roggeveen, Jacob, 21

Saba, 81–82
Sacoahuaman, 14–15; *illus.*, 19
Sagan, Dr. Carl, 95
Sahara Desert, 90–92
Salem (New Hampshire), 49
Salisbury Plain, 53–57
Santa Barbara (California), 47
Sautuola, Don Marcelino de, 59–61
Sequoya, 50
Shell mounds, 44–45
Silbury Hill, 57–58
Silverberg, Robert, *Lost Cities and Vanished Civilizations*, 79
Solomon, King 81
South America, antiquities in, 1–20
Spain, antiquities in, 59–62
Stephens, John Lloyd, 41
Stirling, Dr. Matthew W., 36–37
Stone, Robert, 49
Stonehenge, 53–55; *illus.*, 55
Stonehenge mounds, 56
Sumerians, 79–81

Tarapacá (Chile), 4
Tassili-n-Ajjer cave paintings, (Algeria), 90–92
Temple of the Sun (Cuzco), 14
Tenochtitlán (Mexico), 34
Tiahuanaco, 7–11
Tigris River, 75
Tikal, 42
"Time Capsule," 1939, 97–98
Titicaca, Lake, 7, 11
Toltec antiquities, *illus.*, 42
Tomas, Andrew, 43
Tower of Babel, 78
Twain, Mark, 69

United States, antiquities in, 44–50
Urubamba River, 17

Verrill, Hyatt, 34
Verrill, Ruth, 34
Vimanas, 85–90
Von Hagen, Victor, 40
  Aztec: Man and Tribe, 34

Watusis, 92
Westbury White Horse (England), *illus.*, 59
Westinghouse Time Capsule, 1939, 97–98
Wilkins, Harold T., 34
Windover Hill (Sussex), 58

Yucatán, antiquities in, 41–44

Ziggurat, 78
Zimbabwe (Rhodesia), 83–85

ABOUT THE AUTHOR

Elwood D. Baumann was born in Saskatchewan, Canada, and is a graduate of the University of Wisconsin. After many years as a teacher and principal in schools in Venezuela and eastern Turkey, he took up writing as a vocation and travel as an avocation. He has now traveled in 105 countries on six continents.

Mr. Baumann is a persistent investigator of the unknown. He has lived in the Scottish Highlands and written about the Loch Ness monster. He is an enthusiastic member of the North American Wildlife Research Association and firmly believes in Bigfoot, America's Abominable Snowman, and has delved into the fascinating mysteries surrounding the Devil's Triangle. His engrossing accounts of all three phenomena are published by Franklin Watts.

PROPERTY OF
HOISINGTON JUNIOR HIGH SCHOOL